QUANTUM PRAYER

TEN SCIENTIFIC PRINCIPLES OF ANSWERED PRAYER

STEVE MCVEY

TWS | THE WRITER'S SOCIETY PUBLISHING

TWS | The Writer's Society Publishing
Lodi, CA
www.thewriterssociety.online

Contents

Introduction

The study of quantum mechanics has revolutionized our understanding of the universe at the smallest scales, revealing a world that is stranger and more mysterious than we ever imagined. In this realm, particles can exist in multiple places at once, communicate instantaneously across vast distances, and exhibit wave-particle duality, among other strange phenomena. The principles of quantum mechanics have been verified through countless experiments, and the technology developed from this field has transformed our lives in numerous ways, from computer chips to medical imaging.

However, the implications of quantum mechanics go beyond just technology and physics. The principles of quantum mechanics might also have something to say about our consciousness and faith. This is where the idea of quantum prayer comes in. In the chapters that follow, I would like to challenge you to consider the idea of quantum prayer by showing how particular quantum phenomena have a direct link to prayer when properly understood.

Quantum prayer is a concept that suggests that by understanding how these phenomena can be appropriated in the way we pray, we can see answers to prayers in an unprecedented way. Quantum theory has proven that our thoughts, desires and intentions can collapse the wave function of particles, determining where they exist in space and time. Things that have existed inside the Kingdom of God can manifest in the details of our daily circumstances. Quantum knowledge overturns the outdated scientific belief that everything exists independently of other things and demonstrates that nothing is separate from everything else because all things exist inside the same field of energy, often called the matrix.

This is the same message taught in the Bible, although the Scripture uses the language of faith instead of the language of science. Each subject considered here will be filtered through the lens of Scripture to show its correlation to our faith. What you will see is that the ubiquitous presence of energy that modern science describes is nothing less than the presence of God interacting with all His creation through the union He shares with all things. The Bible explains, "Everything was created through him and for him. He existed before anything else, and he holds all creation together" (COLOSSIANS 1:16-17, NLT).

The strange thing that baffles some quantum researchers is that this nascent metaphysical science acts at times as if this matrix has a mind and will of its own. Albert Einstein described this cosmic vibration of energy that fills everything as "a mysterious tune, intoned in the distance by an invisible piper." Many others use the phrase "cosmic consciousness" to describe this piper referenced by Einstein. Christ-followers use the biblical title, God.

While the idea of quantum prayer might seem far-fetched if your only paradigm has been one built in church, the evidence is solid. By the time you finish these chapters, you will be prepared to pray in a new way, a biblical way animated by truth about how the Creator has designed His creation to work.

Chapter 1

Non-Locality and the Spirit

Throughout history, many religious and philosophical traditions have explored the nature of consciousness and its relationship to God. One idea that runs deep in many of these traditions is the notion that consciousness is not simply a byproduct of physical processes but is, instead, the very essence of God's presence that permeates everything in existence.

This perspective goes so far as to suggest that the fundamental nature of consciousness can't be understood apart from the presence of God. They are the same. The idea that human consciousness is an expression of the presence and mind of God has long been a stream of thought in many religions.

For example, St. Bonaventure, a 13th-century Franciscan mystic and Christian theologian, wrote, "God is a circle whose center is

everywhere and whose circumference is nowhere." The Bhagavad
Gita, a sacred text of the Hindus, says, "I am the Self, O Gudakesa,
seated in the hearts of all creatures. I am the beginning, the
middle, and the end of all beings." The Buddhist text, the
Dhammapada, says, "Mind precedes all mental states. Mind is
their chief; they are all mind-wrought." Jewish rabbis have all
proclaimed the words of the prophet Jeremiah: "'Am I only a God
nearby,' declares the Lord, 'and not a God far away? Who can hide
in secret places so that I cannot see them?' declares the Lord. 'Do
not I fill heaven and earth?' declares the Lord" (JEREMIAH 23:23-
24). The Islamic Koran asserts, "He is Allah, the One and Only;
Allah, the Eternal, Absolute." (QUR'AN 112:1-2)

The prospect of a cosmic consciousness that might be called
"God" seems to be something people know intuitively, regardless
of what religion they embrace. Even an ancient Greek
philosopher, Parmenides, who lived five centuries before Christ,
said, "There is one universal, pervasive, immortal, all-knowing, all-
powerful Being, and that Being is consciousness." Parmenides
argued that reality is composed of a single, unchanging substance
that is eternal and indivisible. He believed that this substance,
which he called "Being," was the only actual reality and that all
other things, including the natural world and our perception of it,
were mere illusions.

A CHRISTOLOGICAL PERSPECTIVE

I make no pretense here that I intend to be neutral about this
topic. As a devoted follower of Jesus Christ, I respect the view of

others. I certainly appreciate their confession of the belief that the consciousness filling all things is God. However, I will go further by saying that this Cosmic Consciousness is a Person known as Christ, the second Person of the Trinity. The Scripture says, "For in him all things were created: things in heaven and on earth, visible and invisible, whether thrones or powers or rulers or authorities; all things have been created through him and for him. He is before all things, and in him all things hold together." (COLOSSIANS 1:16-17, NIV) The Apostle Paul described Him as "the very one who ascended higher than all the heavens, in order to fill the whole universe." (EPHESIANS 4:10, NIV)

Quantum science suggests that our individual experience of consciousness may be connected to this larger, non-local consciousness that pervades all of existence. It postulates that the universe is interconnected in a way that goes beyond what can be explained by classical physics. It suggests that a deeper level of reality may transcend the physical. Many people are not hesitant to call that a spiritual dimension. Modern science points beyond the material world to a metaphysical world that won't fit classical physics. Consciousness is not something that can be understood by the empirical methods science is accustomed to using. Still, they don't deny it is real. It can't be dismissed just because it won't fit the template of scientific materialism of yesteryear.

Nobel laureate physicist, Eugene Wigner, expressed where scientists have found themselves: "It was not possible to formulate the laws of quantum mechanics in a fully consistent way without reference to consciousness . . . The concept of consciousness forces us to revise the classical idea of reality since classical concepts are inadequate to describe phenomena whose existence depends on the involvement of the observer." [1]

Wigner affirms that our individual experience of consciousness may be connected to a non-local consciousness fundamental to a correct interpretation of reality. He suggests that our understanding will only be complete by considering consciousness' role in shaping our perceptions and experiences.

What is this greater consciousness to which he refers? Indeed, it would be a misnomer to call it "consciousness" apart from personhood. However, this isn't just any person but one who encompasses everything. None could reasonably argue that "God" isn't the logical word to use in this instance.

Amit Goswami is a theoretical physicist who has written extensively about the intersection of science and spirituality. In his book *The Self-Aware Universe: How Consciousness Creates the Material World*, Goswami presents the idea that consciousness is the fundamental basis of reality and that the universe is created and sustained by a divine consciousness that he calls "God." Although he is a Hindu, it would seem that Goswami was driven to become a theist by science. [2]

> Believers in Christ would approach any study of
> ultimate reality using a Christological lens.
> Apart from Christ, there is no understanding
> of the cosmos. The Scripture says it is Christ
> "through whom all things came and through
> whom we live." (1 CORINTHIANS 8:6)

Quantum non-locality proposes that everything is interconnected and that the consciousness you experience is the result of being joined together with a larger, non-local consciousness that pervades all of existence. Physicist and philosopher, David Bohm, said, "At the sub-quantum level, everything is interconnected, and that means everything. The entire universe is enfolded in everything, and each thing is enfolded in the whole. This enfoldment is a dynamic process, for all the particles in the universe are constantly in a state of flux." [3]

Your consciousness isn't created inside your brain but is *connected* to a greater Consciousness that fills all things. This connection may be fundamental to our understanding of ourselves and our place in the world. To paraphrase that in the language of a Christian's faith: All of us are joined to the same God who fills everything, and we must understand the meaning and implications of that connection to know ourselves and why we are here.

· · ·

When the Bible says "we have the mind of Christ" in 1 Corinthians 2:16, most haven't seen the quantum nature of that verse. Now we understand it more clearly because of quantum research on consciousness. We do have the mind of Christ in a very literal sense. Your consciousness is a finite, attenuated expression of the very consciousness of Christ. You have the very mind of Christ!

Rumi, a 13th-century Persian mystic, touched the subject when he wrote, "You are not a drop in the ocean. You are the entire ocean in a drop." It's true. You aren't the whole Ocean, but the essence of the entire Ocean dwells in you. To quote the Apostle Paul, "Christ in you, the hope of glory."

NEURONS IN THE MIND OF CHRIST

Consider the way the brain works. When we have a thought, signals pass between brain cells called neurons. Neurons are like messengers that send these signals to one another through electrical and chemical impulses. These signals create a network of activity that underlies our thoughts, emotions, and behaviors. The specific pattern of neuronal activity that occurs with each thought is determined by the particular pathways and connections activated in the brain, which are shaped by our experiences, thoughts, and behaviors.

Generally speaking, every thought you have causes a neuron to fire. When they fire together, they create a synaptic pathway joining the neurons and giving you your conscious experience of life. Now imagine this: All of us are a part of the all-encompassing consciousness of Christ. Remember: "You have the mind of Christ." Are you Christ in His totality? Of course you are not, but you are "the entire ocean in a drop." "For in Him dwells all the fullness of the Godhead bodily, and you are complete in Him." (COLOSSIANS 2:9-10, NKJV) His mind is your mind to be appropriated inside the limits of your finite human experience.

What if, together, we are each a neuron firing inside the mind of Christ? What if Christ expresses His life through His mystical body living in this world today? What if God is experiencing and expressing life through you? This is more than a possibility. It is a fact. The Apostle Paul once wrote, "I no longer live but Christ lives in me. The life that I now live in this body, I live by the faith of the Son of God." (GALATIANS 2:20) Did there cease to be a differentiation between Paul and Christ? No, he still retained his human identity, but he was more than human. The divine life of the Son of God indwelled him. He had the mind of Christ, and Christ lived His life through Paul.

> The Apostle Paul was no anomaly. The same is
> true of you. Non-locality inside the context of
> your faith explains the idea that the Cosmic
> Consciousness of Christ that fills all things has
> simultaneously taken up residence in you and
> is expressed through you and as you. You are
> not alone in this world, left to try to do your

best as you navigate your seven or eight
decades here. "In Him, you live and move and
exist," says the New Testament.

In John 16:17, Jesus told His disciples, "But very truly I tell you, it
is for your good that I am going away. Unless I go away, the
Advocate will not come to you; but if I go, I will send him to you."
The word "Advocate" is the Greek word *Paraclete*. The word
comes from the Greek word *parakletos*, which is a compound of
two words: *para*, which means "beside" or "alongside," and *kletos*,
which means "called" or "summoned." Thus, the word *parakletos*
can be translated as "one who is called alongside" or "one who is
summoned to help or assist."

Is the *Paraclete* in the temporal world or the transcendent world?
Yes, quantum non-locality explains the Spirit being there and yet
here because, in the quantum world, there is no here and there.
Instead, the two somehow mystically merge inside one Unified
Reality. The concept of non-locality in the quantum world
challenges our classical understanding of space and time. It
suggests there may be a deeper level of interconnectedness in the
universe than we have known.

In a later chapter, we will examine the quantum phenomenon
known as superposition, a state where particles can simultaneously
exist in multiple locations or states at once. That describes the

exact relationship of the Spirit to humanity. As theologian Thomas Merton observed, "God is both the Beyond and the Here and Now, both the Other and the Same." [4]

Quantum non-locality has profound implications for our understanding of the role of the Holy Spirit in our lives. The Spirit is sometimes described as an unseen force that permeates all creation and connects us to a greater, transcendent reality. Through manifestations of spiritual gifts, inner promptings, and divine guidance, the Holy Spirit demonstrates a kind of non-locality that points to a deeper level of interconnectedness and consciousness.

This connection between the mind of Christ in the person of His Spirit and your own mind is the starting place for developing a life of prayer sourced far and above the religious routines of prayer we may have been previously taught. Quantum prayer is an expression of His mind being expressed through your prayers. It is to pray in resonance with His intention. The non-locality of His mind gives Complete Knowledge and Perfect Wisdom; praying originates from the heart of God as His Spirit activates and animates your prayers. The expression of His mind through you brings supernatural potential because of the supernatural origin of the prayer.

Through our faith and relationship with Christ, we can tap into this higher Consciousness and experience a greater sense of purpose and meaning in our prayers. This kind of prayer isn't trying to persuade God to do something we want and now must convince Him to do; quantum prayer aligns us with what He wants. To quote Martin Luther: "Prayer is not overcoming God's reluctance. It is laying hold of His willingness." Quantum prayer isn't you reaching up to God. It is the Spirit moving inside the eternal realm through your external requests in prayer. When you pray, the universe is already tilted in your favor.

The Bible says in Romans 8:26-27, "Likewise the Spirit also helps in our weaknesses. For we do not know what we should pray for as we ought, but the Spirit Himself makes intercession for us with groanings which cannot be uttered. Now He who searches the hearts knows what the mind of the Spirit is because He makes intercession for the saints according to the will of God." This passage suggests that when we struggle to find the words, or know what to pray for, the Holy Spirit intercedes on our behalf, communicating with God in ways that may be beyond our understanding. It's a mystical process involving the Holy Spirit, who may communicate with God in ways beyond human words or comprehension.

> You have the mind of Christ and are an expression
> of His life in an attenuated form. This means
> that you are connected to the divine
> consciousness that permeates all of creation
> and have access to a higher level of awareness
> beyond your individual experiences. Through

Him, you can tap into this higher
Consciousness and experience a greater sense
of purpose and meaning in life.

When we see how these concepts integrate inside quantum non-locality, we begin to understand that our lives, indeed, are part of a larger, interconnected whole that transcends our individual experiences. We aren't just individually praying, but rather are integral parts of the Kingdom of God that are interconnected and mutually interactive. The seen and unseen worlds work together on our behalf when we pray as the Spirit directs at every level.

The idea that our lives are part of a larger, interconnected whole is a powerful reminder of the possibilities in the universe and the transformative power of quantum prayer. When we see non-locality through our spiritual eyes and its implications for our spiritual lives, we can begin to tap into a deeper level of awareness and consciousness that elevates and empowers our prayer life. We can align ourselves with the mind of Christ and open ourselves up to the infinite possibilities that exist.

As we continue to explore the mysteries of the quantum world and our own spiritual experiences, you may find that the boundaries between the physical and spiritual realms are not as clear-cut as once thought and that the Holy Spirit is at work in ways that transcend your current understanding.

CHAPTER 2

ENTANGLEMENT AND UNION WITH CHRIST

Non-locality and quantum entanglement are two related concepts in the world of physics. While non-locality speaks to the interconnectedness of all things, quantum entanglement takes it a step further. Non-locality refers to a situation where two particles can be far apart, but measuring one particle can instantly affect the other particle's state. This is unusual because there is no physical way for the particles to communicate with each other, yet they seem to be connected in a way that classical physics can't explain.

Quantum entanglement is a specific example of non-locality, in which two particles become linked so that the state of one particle not only influences but defines the other particle's state. This means that measuring the state of one particle will instantly reveal the other particle's state, even if they are far apart. In some mysterious way, they are "in union" and sharing information instantaneously, even though they may seem to be separated in time and space.

If non-locality explains the nearness of the Paraclete to us, entanglement zooms in on the idea and brings us to the indication of the oneness that exists between God and us. When two particles become entangled, their identities somehow merge and become part of a single quantum system, and, as strange as it seems, the two become one. Spin one particle in a counterclockwise direction, and the other will instantly move the same way, whether six inches apart or six lightyears apart. Spin it clockwise, and the other will simultaneously do the same. One doesn't just influence the other but is in some way mysteriously in union with it.

> It's a weird concept that baffles even the most educated and experienced scientists. No less brilliant mind than Albert Einstein called entanglement "spooky action that happens at a distance." It makes no sense, and yet it's true. Michio Kaku, a theoretical physicist and popular science communicator, had this to say about it: "It is often stated that of all the theories proposed in this century, the silliest is quantum theory. Some say that the only thing that quantum theory has going for it, in fact, is that it is unquestionably correct." [1]

Two particles are somehow one. The statement itself sounds contradictory. How can two be one? How can one particle be in two places at the same time? It's mind-boggling, but it's true. The exciting thing is that this strange phenomenon is a perfect picture of your relationship with God.

YOUR ENTANGLEMENT WITH CHRIST MEANS UNION WITH GOD

Emmanuel means "God with us," but the Apostle Paul championed an idea we now understand not only to be theological but scientific. "Christ in you, the hope of glory," is how he described it. It's not just God *with* you but *in* you. This is a clear biblical expression of quantum entanglement. Be sure to note what was said about the meaning of quantum entanglement previously. "Two particles become linked in such a way that the state of one particle defines the state of the other particle." They are in union but manifest in two places simultaneously, and one defines the other. What a picture of Christ and you!

The incarnation of Jesus Christ is the visible evidence that God has joined Himself in union with us. In the Old Testament scriptures, the Bible sometimes speaks of how "the Spirit of the Lord came mightily" upon Samson, Saul, David, and others. When that happened, they were miraculously empowered for a particular purpose. That empowerment is a beautiful picture of non-locality in demonstrating how the influence of one particle (or, in this case, a Person) can influence another.

. . .

However, in the New Testament, the Bible teaches that it's even better now. The Spirit resides in you. God doesn't come upon you at certain moments to help you. The Spirit of Christ does more than lead you; the Spirit lives in you. In 1 Corinthians 6:19, the Apostle Paul asked, "Do you not know that your body is the temple of the Holy Spirit who is in you?"

In an interview with *Discover Magazine*, quantum physicist John Wheeler said, "The idea of two physically separated particles exhibiting instantaneous correlations seems strange because we have a built-in idea of locality. But what we call entanglement is just another way of talking about the fact that we have one system, and we describe the whole system with one wave function. There's really only one entity."

Wheeler is emphasizing here the idea that entangled particles are not separate entities but actually one. He suggests that the behavior of entanglement seems strange because of our limited perspective based on the concept of locality. It's our perspective that objects can only affect each other through direct physical interactions. However, particles can be so closely connected in quantum mechanics that they are somehow one, even though there is still differentiation within that oneness. This is an excellent scientific description of the relationship between you and the Christ who indwells you.

. . .

You are not Christ, and Christ is not you, yet there is a sense in which you certainly are one. "But he who is joined to the Lord is one spirit with him," we're told in 1 Corinthians 6:17. Your union with Christ doesn't eradicate your identity, but what it does do is merge your identity into His. Paul the Apostle explained it by saying, "My old self has been crucified with Christ. It is no longer I who live, but Christ lives in me." (GALATIANS 2:20, NLT) Then, later in the same verse, he says, "I live in this earthly body by trusting in the Son of God, who loved me and gave himself for me." So, who was living that lifestyle? Was it Paul or Christ? The answer is, "Yes, it was One and both" because of union.

The Apostle Peter affirmed that we have been made able "to share his divine nature." (2 PETER 1:4, NLT) That's nothing less than quantum entanglement, as described by various experts. For instance, John Polkinghorne (1930-2021) was a British theoretical physicist, theologian, and Anglican priest. He studied at the University of Cambridge, earning a Ph.D. in physics, and later became a professor of mathematical physics. Polkinghorne made significant contributions to particle physics and quantum field theory before leaving academia to become an ordained priest in the Church of England. In addition, he became a prolific writer on the relationship between science and religion. Here's what he said about the subject: "When two particles are entangled, their states become interdependent such that the state of one particle is defined by the state of the other." [2]

Science writer Jennifer Ouellette wrote, "When

two particles are entangled, they become a
single system with a shared quantum state.
That means the state of one particle cannot be
defined without reference to the other
particle's state. So, if you measure the state of
one particle, you can instantly know the state
of the other particle, no matter how far apart
they are." [3]

In his book, *Fundamentals: Ten Keys to Reality*, Frank Wilczek
wrote, "Entanglement is a correlation between particles that is so
strong that they become inseparable. In other words, their
quantum states are defined by each other." [4]

Let's apply this powerful scientific reality to your relationship with
Christ and how it affects prayer. He defines you. You are
inseparably joined with Him in a way that His nature has become
yours. How does that translate into quantum prayer? The
quantum entanglement you share with Jesus Christ defines you in
several powerful ways that will affect your prayers.

YOU ARE WORTHY OF HAVING YOUR PRAYERS ANSWERED

Legalistic religion always leaves a person with a sense of deficiency.
No matter how much you do, it's never enough. Do more. Try
harder. Rededicate yourself. It's still not enough. The indictments

and demands seem endless. Legalism is a system of living in which a person tries to make spiritual progress or gain God's blessings based on what he does. It is a futile attempt to achieve a state of worthiness and isn't even necessary.

Grace is a system of living in which a person is blessed because they are in Christ and for no other reason. You are under grace, so you don't have to struggle to achieve anything. Instead, you can simply receive the reality that God loves and accepts you just as you are right now. The King James Version of the Bible states it beautifully in Ephesians 1:6, in saying, "To the praise of the glory of his grace, wherein he hath made us accepted in the beloved."

"The beloved" is Christ. You are entangled with Him, so the fact is that you are as accepted by God the Father as Jesus Christ is. Don't think it's prideful to recognize that you are worthy of having your prayers answered. It's because of Him. He defines you to the Father. If you don't deserve to have prayers answered, neither does Jesus. *You are defined by Him.* Let that sink in, and it will transform you. Understanding the implications of quantum entanglement to your relationship with Christ will change your prayer life.

YOU ARE A CHILD OF GOD

In Matthew 7:9-11, when Jesus was teaching about prayer, here's what He said: "Which of you if your son asks for bread, will give him a stone? Or if he asks for a fish, will give him a snake? If you, then, though you are evil, know how to give good gifts to your children, how much more will your Father in heaven give good gifts to those who ask him!" (NIV)

When Paul spoke on Mars Hill, he made a striking statement pointing to the entanglement you are with Christ. He said, "'For in him we live and move and have our being.' As some of your own poets have said, 'We are his offspring.'" (ACTS 17:28, NIV) Remember the quantum reality that when two particles are entangled, they become a single system with a shared quantum state. That's science-speak. Paul says it here: "In Him, we live and move and have our being." Do you see that he's saying the same thing?

Then Paul goes on to say, "We are his offspring." In the Interlinear Bible, the Greek word used in Acts 17:28 for "offspring" is γένος (*genos*), which can be translated as "family" or "child." The word is the root of "genealogy." Does knowing that you have the very DNA of Christ in you encourage you about the power of quantum prayer? It should!

You don't have to beg God to answer your prayers. You are His child, and just as all good parents want to be loving and generous to their own children, your Father wants to be good to you. There is never a moment when your Father's heart is not for you. You come from His genealogy, therefore you can pray with confidence.

YOU HAVE THE MIND OF CHRIST

1 Corinthians 2:16 (NASB) says, "For who has known the mind of the Lord, that he will instruct Him? But we have the mind of Christ." Not only does this verse suggest that we know the thoughts God has, but it specifically states that we have the mind of Christ. Quantum entanglement allows us to know how that works. Paul's words in this text aren't metaphorical and ought not to be spiritualized so that they lose their meaning.

You share the mind of Christ. That doesn't mean there aren't conflicting thoughts that come to you from what the Bible calls "the world, the flesh, and the devil," but it does mean that you are in a state defined by His thoughts. As you depend on Christ, He will guide your thought process as you pray. Imagine the power that gives to your prayers! This is all a result of the entangled mind you share with Him.

This Bible text is relatively simple in most Bible translations, but one paraphrase seems to explode with enthusiasm when addressing this idea.

The Message renders I Corinthians 2:9-16
this way:

"No one's ever seen or heard anything like this,

Never so much as imagined anything quite
    like it—
What God has arranged for those who love him.
But you've seen and heard it because God, by his
    Spirit, has brought it all out into the open
    before you.
The Spirit, not content to flit around on the
    surface, dives into the depths of God and
    brings out what God planned all along. Who
    ever knows what you're thinking and planning
    except you yourself? The same with God—
    except that he not only knows what he's
    thinking, but he lets us in on it. God offers a
    full report on the gifts of life and salvation
    that he is giving us. We don't have to rely on
    the world's guesses and opinions. We didn't
    learn this by reading books or going to school;
    we learned it from God, who taught us
    person-to-person through Jesus, and we're
    passing it on to you in the same firsthand,
    personal way.

The unspiritual self, just as it is by nature, can't
    receive the gifts of God's Spirit. There's no
    capacity for them. They seem like so much
    silliness. Spirit can be known only by spirit—
    God's Spirit and our spirits in open
    communion. Spiritually alive, we have access
    to everything God's Spirit is doing and can't
    be judged by unspiritual critics. Isaiah's

question, "Is there anyone around who knows
God's Spirit, anyone who knows what he is
doing?" has been answered: Christ knows, and
we have Christ's Spirit."

"Christ knows, and we have Christ's Spirit." Your mind is
entangled with His mind. Take that into your prayer life and
watch what happens! This is quantum prayer in its purest form.

YOU CAN PRAY WITH THE FAITH OF CHRIST

The implications of quantum entanglement in your relationship
with God affect every area of life, but nowhere does it impact your
prayers more than in the area of faith. The union you share with
Him is the basis for sharing His very nature. Inherent to sharing
the nature of Christ is the reality that you share His faith. Think
about that: He doesn't help build your faith but gives you His
faith. One Bible verse, in particular, makes this reality evident. The
King James Version is the most on-target translation of Galatians
2:20. While many translations suggest living by faith in Christ, the
KJV says this: "I am crucified with Christ: nevertheless, I live; yet
not I, but Christ liveth in me: and the life which I now live in the
flesh I live by the faith of the Son of God, who loved me and gave
himself for me."

The New Testament was first written in Greek. The original
language is especially important to this text. Did Paul say that he

lived *by faith in* the Son of God, as many translations suggest, or did he say that he lived *by the faith of* the Son of God, as the King James Bible says? In Greek, the genitive possessive is a grammatical case that indicates a relationship of possession or belonging between two nouns. It is similar to the possessive case in English, where an apostrophe and an "s" are added to a noun to show ownership (e.g., Steve's book). That's how Paul said it in this verse. He literally wrote: "I live by the Son of God's faith." The text doesn't indicate that he directed his faith toward Christ but rather that he lived by Christ's faith. Do you see the difference that makes?

When you pray, your prayers aren't empowered by your own ability to work up faith, but instead, your prayers are empowered by the faith of Christ Himself. You can approach God without doubt or uncertainty and move into a place where you can see miraculous answers manifest in your life because of the faith of Christ.

You Can Pray Without a Victim Mentality

The powerful scientific reality of quantum entanglement not only enables us to pray with the faith of Christ but also allows us to pray without a victim mentality. In our union with Christ, we're no longer defined by our past mistakes, failures, or circumstances. Instead, we are defined by God's love, grace, and acceptance for us in Him. This understanding frees us from the mindset that we are powerless victims, continually at the mercy of life's challenges and struggles.

. . .

When you pray without a victim mentality, you approach God with an understanding of your true identity as His beloved child. You recognize that you aren't helpless or hopeless but are empowered by the Holy Spirit within you. As a result, you can confidently ask for God's response, knowing you are worthy of His love and attention. In this state of mind, your prayers become bold declarations of faith, affirming the truth of your divine nature and your union with God through Christ. This shift in perspective allows you to fully embrace quantum prayer's power, transforming your life and circumstances.

The fantastic reality of entanglement in physics offers an incredible illustration of your spiritual union with God. As you embrace your union with Christ, it will revolutionize your prayer life. Your quantum entanglement with Jesus defines your worthiness, confirms your identity as a child of God, and gives you the mind of Christ. This powerful connection enables you to approach prayer with confidence and assurance, fully aware of the divine resources available to you. Apply the truth quantum entanglement teaches and allow the transformative power of quantum prayer to bring you into the fullness of all God has for you.

CHAPTER 3

SUPERPOSITION AND SEEING THE SUPERNATURAL

Some things in the Bible that seem contradictory and hard to understand at first glance are made clear through the quantum lens. For example, the Bible teaches that Christ is seated at the right hand of the Father but also says that He is here with us at every moment. Which is it? Is He here or there?

Then there's Ephesians 2:6, which says, "God raised us up with Christ and seated us with him in the heavenly realms in Christ Jesus." (NIV) So, do we live here on earth, or are we, too, there in the heavenly realms with Jesus Christ?

One more example, focusing on prayer: On the one hand, we are told that we have been given everything we need for life (2 PETER 1:3), and on the other, Jesus said, "Ask, and it will be given to you." (MATTHEW 7:7 NIV) Do we or don't we already have what we need?

Other biblical examples seem to say two different things. Thankfully, because of the explanation from quantum science, we can understand how these paradoxical passages don't contradict but fit together perfectly. Science can complement our faith at this point.

In the quantum world, superposition refers to the phenomenon in which a particle exists simultaneously in multiple states or positions until focus is placed on it. Then the particle manifests as a single and definite outcome. Like other quantum phenomena, it's a strange thing counterintuitive to our usual logical reasoning. Something being in two places at one time? Nobel Prize-winning physicist Richard Feynman affirmed the weirdness of the whole thing when he said, "Do not keep asking yourself, if you can possibly avoid it, 'But how can it be like that?' because you will get 'down the drain,' into a blind alley from which nobody has yet escaped. Nobody knows how it can be like that." [1]

The thing you're praying for already exists. Every outcome does. How can every outcome exist outside time and space so that any of them is a possibility for us? As the esteemed scientist said, "Nobody knows how it can be like that."

But Jesus said it is indeed like that: "All things are possible to him who believes," and "All things are possible with God." His words are about as clear as can be. Every answer to your prayers already exists with God. It's real and only needs to be realized.

Reconsider the previous questions. Understanding the meaning of superposition causes these biblical dilemmas to make sense. Is Christ seated at the right hand of His Father in heaven, or is He here? The answer is both. How about us? Are we seated with Him in the heavenly realm, as the Bible teaches, or are we on planet Earth? The answer is yes, it's both. So, when it comes to prayer, what about asking so that we may receive what we need? Do we ask, or do we already have what we need? Again, the answer is both. Trying to understand that fact can almost feel maddening to the rational mind. It seems logical that either we do or we don't.

LEAVING A DUALISTIC MIND

One reason is that human logic grounded in a dualistic mindset that suggests things must be either/or misses the point on some important spiritual matters. Outside the linear boundaries of time and space is a world of both/and. For example, do you have or not have the answer to your prayers? The answer doesn't have to be yes or no, but, in a sense, it can be both. Yes, God has already given you everything you need, but no, you don't always immediately see it in your circumstances. An essential step toward answered prayers is learning to see not only the temporal reality we perceive with our senses but also to see the supernatural reality we perceive in our spirits. The latter is more real than the former. "So we fix our eyes not on what is seen, but on what is unseen, since what is seen is temporary, but what is unseen is eternal" (2 CORINTHIANS 4:18)

The Bible explains, "Now all we can see of God is like a cloudy picture . . ." (1 CORINTHIANS 13:12, CEV) Remember that outcomes in superposition are in wave form, a blurry state, not having manifested in spacetime as a specific result. We need to see at a level deeper than our finite brains allow. We need to see from the core of our beings. The Apostle Paul prayed for this very experience for his Ephesian friends. He wrote to them, "And [I pray] that the eyes of your heart [the very center and core of your being] may be enlightened [flooded with light by the Holy Spirit] so that you will know and cherish the hope [the divine guarantee, the confident expectation] to which He has called you." (EPHESIANS 1:18, AMPLIFIED BIBLE) Seeing with the eyes of your heart. That's the gateway to answered prayer.

Superposition presents an objective reality that is as absolute as anything could be despite existing in an indistinct state. It is finished and is yet to be manifested. You may think it's just a mind game to act as if something is real that hasn't been realized, but it's actually a matter of learning to see beyond the temporal world and into the transcendent world where every outcome resides.

· · ·

The Copenhagen interpretation of quantum
mechanics is one way to understand the
strange rules of the quantum world. It says
that tiny particles like electrons exist in a state
of probability until we measure or observe
them, at which point they pop into a definite
place. The outcome already exists, but it
resides in another dimension until it
materializes in our experience. So, also, has
your prayer already been answered inside the
Kingdom of God. In this world, things exist in
two places: the metaphysical and the physical.
To see physically, it is simply a matter of
manifestation.

I know. It sounds like science fiction. Theoretical physicist Sabine
Hossenfelder agrees. In her book, *Lost in Math: How Beauty Leads
Physics Astray*, she wrote, "It's a story so crazy that if you tried to
sell it as science fiction, no one would buy it." [2]

If you want to take a great stride forward toward seeing your
prayers answered, you need to wrap your heart around this truth
even when you can't wrap your brain around it. You have already
been given everything you need. It's done. That's what the Bible
says, and there's no ambiguity in how it's stated: "His divine

power has given us everything we need for life." The Apostle Peter couldn't have been more straightforward.

> Don't let some connection you make with
> something you've heard from a New Ager or
> an over-the-top religious zealot cause you to
> reject this. This is neither a cultish viewpoint
> nor a name-it-and-claim-it religious formula.
> Just because it has been misappropriated
> incorrectly doesn't negate the truth. You may
> be tempted to say, "That sounds like . . ." and
> then connect it to something that would cause
> you to deny it. Please don't do that, because
> it's real. Jesus said it. The Apostle Peter said it.
> Paul said it. Science says it. Don't let a knee-
> jerk reaction cause you to miss it because of
> some misguided characterization you may be
> tempted to assign based on guilt by
> association.

This present-tense-perspective will first change you, then change your circumstances. You don't have to fully understand it to believe it. Think of the things you already believe to be true even though it doesn't look that way when you judge by what you can see through human rationale: Christ has conquered sin, but you wouldn't think so if you go by what you see in the world. God loves humanity, but you wouldn't believe it if you judged the matter solely by the human suffering you can observe. We are one in Christ, but looking at forty-five-thousand-plus Christian denominations wouldn't suggest so. Heaven is your home, but you've never laid eyes on it. You are created in the image of Christ but self-examination through human understanding might challenge that reality.

The things mentioned in the previous paragraphs are true, and most followers of Christ believe them, even when logic dictates otherwise. This is the place we need to come to on prayer. Your answer isn't something God needs to do. He has done all He is going to do and has given it all to you in Christ. The answer rests in discovering who we are and what we possess in Him.

"Superposition" in the quantum world and "supernatural" in the world of faith both point to the same reality, a reality that exists above classical physics and linear, legalistic religion. They point to that dimension that human eyes can't see, a dimension that transcends and transforms the physical world.

Contemporary descriptions have referred to this transcendent world as the divine matrix, the field, Universe, and Source. Jesus referred to it as the Kingdom of God. When Paul spoke of being "in Christ," he meant more than the historical Jesus, although the man Jesus certainly was a perfect and complete manifestation of this Reality. When Paul referred to the One by whom "all things were created that are in heaven and that are on earth, visible and invisible, whether thrones or dominions or principalities or powers," he obviously, wasn't speaking of an impersonal force but of the One who "is before all things, and in [whom] all things consist." (COLOSSIANS 1:16-17, NKJV)

Christ is Ultimate Reality, and everything resides in Him, including every answer to every prayer you ever utter. It's all held in superposition in Christ. Don't make the mistake of thinking this suggests that Christ can be reduced to a scientific explanation. On the contrary, all actual science exists inside Him. Romans 11:36 (ESV) says, "For from Him and through Him and to Him are all things." There is nothing outside of Christ. He is the Creator and Sustainer of everything. Gaining a clear vision of the all-pervasive presence of Christ and recognizing that all you need is in superposition in Him bolsters your faith to pray with confidence and assurance that He has you and all you need. You lack nothing because He lacks nothing. The fullness of Almighty God dwells in Him, and you are complete in Him!

LOOKING BEYOND THE TEMPORAL

One biblical example of someone who saw this divine dimension and was empowered by it is the Apostle John. Exiled on the island of Patmos as punishment for his ministry, John was left alone to serve his sentence in solitude. The Bible records how his sight was opened to look beyond the superficial world and see into the world of superposition, where everything is already settled despite the unsettled sense often accompanying the human experience.

He described what he saw in Revelation 4:1-2:

> "After these things, I looked, and behold a door standing open in heaven, and the first voice which I had heard, like the sound of a trumpet speaking with me, said, 'Come up here, and I will show you what must take place after these things.' Immediately I was in the Spirit; and behold, a throne was standing in heaven and One sitting on the throne." (NASB)

The first thing that John saw was a door standing open in heaven. What is the significance of this door? A door is a passageway connecting two different places. In this instance, it was a passage between two areas of reality – the natural and the supernatural.

The Spirit called John to enter through this door and to see beyond the natural world into an eternal world. His body was on Patmos, but he could look past the bounds of his physical location and see his spiritual home. John saw that he was living in two worlds at the same time – the material and the spiritual. What a relief that must have been to him.

. . .

There is a sense in which you, too, simultaneously live in dual worlds. If you are to realize the answer to your prayers, it is imperative to look through your finite situation and see the infinite possibilities inside the Kingdom of God. Although things may seem to have brought you to a dead end, there are endless ways you can go forward from here.

Looking at his circumstances, John might have reasonably concluded that the situation was hopeless. But he didn't just look *at* his circumstances; he looked *through* them into the world where the answers already existed in superposition. That spiritual sight gave him the strength to endure.

Confidence in prayer vanishes like dew under the hot sun of Patmos if the only thing we can see is the visible circumstances of our lives. The answer you need is in Christ, in superposition alongside the supernatural. The Bible teaches it to be so. Science teaches it to be true. The experience of many has proven it to be real.

> In which area of reality do you find your life
> absorbed? If your focus is only on the natural
> world, you are suffering from short-
> sightedness. Quantum superposition gives us a
> lens to look beyond the bounds of temporality

and see that there is another world. The eyes
of the heart allow us to see into that world of
the supernatural so that, when the outlook is
bleak, we can practice the up-look!

It's noteworthy that when John saw the throne, Someone was
sitting on it. The fact that He was seated speaks volumes. Your
heavenly Father isn't pacing the corridors of heaven worrying
about how things will be resolved. He's sitting because there's
nothing left to do on your behalf. It has already been done. It is
finished. He's not worrying, so why should you?

Even Max Planck, known as the father of quantum mechanics,
noted this spiritual reality that holds everything together. He
wrote, "As a man who has devoted his whole life to the most clear-
headed science, to the study of matter, I can tell you as a result of
my research about atoms this much: There is no matter as such!
All matter originates and exists only by virtue of a force which
brings the particles of an atom to vibration and holds this most
minute solar system of the atom together . . . We must assume
behind this force the existence of a conscious and intelligent
Mind. This Mind is the matrix of all matter." [3] It doesn't take a
genius to recognize that, without using the word Christ, the Mind
he referenced is Christ Himself. Christ is the Matrix, and the
answers to your prayers are all in Him. What good news!

. . .

Understanding the concept of superposition can give us the eyes to see into the Kingdom of God, where all possibilities reside and every answer to our prayers already exists. As we learn to see through the eyes of our hearts, we begin to trust that even when we can't see or imagine the answers to our prayers, we know that they exist in the realm of possibilities. Quantum prayer allows us to take comfort in the fact that God is always working for our good and that His plans are far greater than anything we could ever imagine.

CHAPTER 4

THE OBSERVER EFFECT AND OUTCOMES

The observer effect is a principle in quantum mechanics that highlights the influence the simple act of observation (or what physicists call measurement) has on a quantum system. It states that the very act of focusing on or interacting with something can change its behavior or even its state. This concept challenges the classical notion that measurements can be made without affecting what is measured. Instead, any attention to something affects it in some way.

The double-slit experiment is one of the most famous examples of the observer effect. When particles, such as electrons or photons, are sent through a barrier with two slits, they exhibit wave-like behavior and create an interference pattern on a screen behind the barrier when they aren't watched. However, when an observer tries to determine which slit the particle passes through, the interference pattern disappears, and the particles act like individual particles instead of waves. They then go through one slit or the other. This change in behavior shows that the act of observing (or measuring) the particles has directly affected their behavior. It seems bizarre that nothing more than putting attention on something can activate a particular outcome.

> Where we place our attention becomes the
> guiding influence for what happens in life and
> certainly can affect how we pray. No wonder
> the Bible instructs us repeatedly to take charge
> of our thoughts and where we direct them.
> Combine what you look at and think about,
> and you have the perfect formula for a specific
> outcome. [1]

The quantum understanding of wave-particle duality is that a subatomic particle can simultaneously exist in two states. It's the act of observation that causes it to collapse into one particular state. Anything can happen, and what you watch will have an inestimable influence on the outcome.

The implications of this truth offer an opportunity to understand and approach prayer in an advantaged way that the world of religion has never proposed. Legalistic religion has many suggestions for seeing prayers answered. Which approach a person takes likely depends on the culture of their religious indoctrination.

QUANTUM PRAYER REPLACES LEGALISTIC PRAYER

Some suggest that prayers are answered when we have praised God enough. Others say it's when we have proven ourselves by our spiritual service. Another view interprets faith as a currency that will cause our prayers to be answered if we have enough. There are many other religious methods people use to try to get their prayers answered. While there is a quantum lens through which these approaches might be interpreted, most of the time, they are things we do to try to get God to do something. In some situations, it would be hard to argue against the charge that they're nothing more than religious ways to try to manipulate God into doing what we want. If I praise, fast, serve, study, give, or do other things prescribed by my particular denomination, I'll be more likely to receive answers to my prayers.

> This legalistic approach revolves around looking at yourself and what you're doing. Answered prayers in that world usually depend on you, leaving you in a never-ending cycle of trying to do better for God so you can get better from God. It's exhausting, and, worst of all, it doesn't work. Answered prayers are hit-and-miss in that linear legalistic lunacy, and it's exhausting, too.

. . .

What if what we've been taught is wrong? What if God isn't waiting for us to do anything before He answers our prayers? What if it isn't a reluctance on His part but a lack of knowledge on our part about how prayer works that keeps our prayers from being answered?

It doesn't matter how sincere a person is in their aim to reach a destination if they're headed in the wrong direction. For example, if you need to go to a city one hundred miles north of you, it won't be possible to get there driving south, regardless of how fast you drive.

FOCUSING IN THE RIGHT PLACE

Let's be clear: Every answer to every prayer you will ever utter resides in Christ. The answer may be yes, no, wait, or something different than you can imagine, but all the answers are in Him. For that reason, the only successful starting place for seeing prayers answered is to understand the importance of keeping your focus on Him. Do you want your prayers answered? Then look to the Source of all the answers. "Looking unto Jesus, the author and finisher of our faith" is the way Hebrews 12:2 describes it. Whatever the outcome, you will want to be aware of the presence of Christ.

. . .

When Israel was being bitten and killed by venomous snakes because of their rebelliousness, it looked hopeless. But then they had a change of heart about their constant complaining and criticism of God and Moses, and asked Moses to pray to God on their behalf to remove the snakes. Moses prayed for them, and God instructed him to make a bronze serpent and place it on a pole. He instructed Moses to tell those bitten by a snake to look at the bronze serpent, and they would be healed and live.

That serpent in the wilderness is a metaphor for Jesus Christ. When you are scared of the "snakes" in your situation, look at Jesus. When the pain is prolonged and powerful, look at Jesus. When there seems to be no way of escape, look at Jesus. Look at Him and know that He is looking at you. He sees your situation and you in it. He wants to teach you to see it through His eyes.

It would probably be fair to say that the greatest need most people have is to focus differently on the situation they are praying about by beginning to see it through this Christological lens. When we can see our condition through the eyes of Christ, things will change, because, if nothing else, we have changed. If you were to be able to see your circumstances through the eyes of Jesus Christ right now, would that affect you?

Jesus Christ is the author – the originator – and the finisher – the one who ensures your faith's completion, including every facet of your life. Before you look at your perceived need, stare into the face of the One who has the ability, desire, and intention to give you precisely what you need. He will not fail you; if you think He has, it's because you haven't cooperated with the way He does things. The observer effect applies even in your relationship with God. God will respond to us, but He will not honor our delusions and misguided notions by blessing our legalistic lunacy.

> It's not enough to be sincere. Sincerity may be admirable, but the Teacher inside us wants us to be straight in the way we think. The Greek word *orthos* means "straight," while *doxa* originally meant "belief." Orthodoxy is straight thinking, and God wants you to be orthodox when it comes to prayer. Look to Him, and He will act. You shall know the truth, and the truth shall set you free.

Start by looking away from your problem for a moment, look at Him, and ask Him to give you eyes to see the truth of the matter. You still may not have the answers you want about the details, but that's okay. Affirm, by the power of grace, that you will begin to reinterpret the subject of your prayer through the lens of Christ's commitment and compassion toward you. There may be much you don't know about the situation of your prayer concern, but one thing you do know is that "Love never fails." (I CORINTHIANS 13:8, NIV) Start by looking upward and inward, not outward. "Set your mind on the things above, not on the things that are on earth" is how Colossians 3:2 explains it. That's not to suggest that we are oblivious to the external world but that we are to be anchored in the eternal world.

C.S. Lewis wrote in *Mere Christianity*, "Aim at Heaven, and you will get Earth 'thrown in'; aim at Earth, and you will get neither." [2] Jesus said the same thing by telling us to seek first the Kingdom of God, and all these other things would then be added. Having set the pillar for prayer as the Person of Christ, we are then able to see our external world through the lens of the eternal world. Temporality is reframed by Transcendence. Circumstances are redefined through Christ.

Science bears out the power of observation in many ways. In addition to the double slit experiment, another intriguing scientific study known as "Wigner's friend" speaks to the subject. This experiment involves Wigner, and his friend, and a quantum particle, such as a photon.

Initially, Wigner's friend is situated inside a sealed laboratory along with the photon, which exists in a superposition of two states. In the last chapter, we discussed how that superposition is the state embodying a combination of various potential outcomes. At the moment of the friend's observation of the photon, its wavefunction collapses, resulting in a single, definite state.

· · ·

Meanwhile, Wigner remains outside the laboratory, unaware of the outcome of his friend's observation. From his perspective, the photon continues to exist in a superposition of states. At this stage, Wigner regards the laboratory, his friend, and the photon as parts of a more extensive quantum system that also exists in a superposition of states.

However, the moment Wigner opens the laboratory and asks about the result, his act of observation causes the entire system, encompassing the laboratory, his friend, and the photon, to collapse into a specific state. This experiment highlights the dynamic role of the observer in determining the outcome of events and emphasizes the complex and paradoxical nature of quantum mechanics.

The man in the laboratory experienced one reality. For a time, the one on the outside experienced another. Choose to enter into the laboratory of Love, fix your eyes on Jesus Christ, and trust that the blurry situation will manifest in the best way possible. To quote one biblical text, you may see "through a glass, darkly," but the quantum world is a field of possibility. It's not a world of control, but as a follower of Christ, you know that the unseen world is a Field of Favor where whatever happens will be the best expression of God's love that He could possibly give you. Set your mind on goodness and grace and wait with expectancy.

CHANGING HOW WE SEE THINGS

Once you have deeply observed Jesus, you will be captured by the awareness of His Life within you, and you will be equipped to look at your circumstances differently. For example, during the experiment with Wigner's friend, two people saw the state of the photon in different ways. The one who had observed it saw it in particle form while Wigner, having not observed it, still could only conceive it in wave form. Only when he changed what he focused on did the situation change for him.

There's a biblical story that brings the power of this observer effect into focus in a helpful way. The story is in 2 Kings 6:8-17. *The Message* tells the story well:

> "One time when the king of Aram was at war with Israel, after consulting with his officers, he said, 'At such and such a place, I want an ambush set.' The Holy Man sent a message to the king of Israel: 'Watch out when you're passing this place because Aram has set an ambush there.'
>
> So the king of Israel sent word concerning the place of which the Holy Man had warned him. This kind of thing happened all the time. The king of Aram was furious over all this. He called his officers together and said, 'Tell me,

who is leaking information to the king of
Israel? Who is the spy in our ranks?'

But one of his men said, 'No, my master, dear
king. It's not any of us. It's Elisha, the prophet
in Israel. He tells the king of Israel everything
you say, even when you whisper it in your
bedroom.'

The king said, 'Go and find out where he is. I'll
send someone and capture him.'

The report came back, 'He's in Dothan.'

Then he dispatched horses and chariots, an
impressive fighting force. They came by night
and surrounded the city. Early in the morning,
a servant of the Holy Man got up and
went out.

Surprise! Horses and chariots surrounding the
city! The young man exclaimed, 'Oh, master!
What shall we do?'

He said, 'Don't worry about it – there are more on
our side than on their side." Then Elisha
prayed, 'O GOD, open his eyes and let him
see.'

The eyes of the young man were opened, and he

saw. A wonder! The whole mountainside full
of horses and chariots of fire surrounding
Elisha!"

Like Wigner and his friend, Elisha and his servant related to the
same experience in two different ways. The variable was where
they looked. Elisha's servant could only see the facts of the
surrounding details in the external world around him. Elisha
wasn't in denial about that, but his observation looked through it
into the eternal world. Looking there caused him to be at peace in
the middle of a situation that would terrify anyone who didn't see
the whole picture.

He prayed for the servant's eyes to be opened, and when they
were, what did he see? "A wonder!" On the one hand, nothing had
changed, and on the other hand, everything had changed. The
observer effect transformed his circumstances by nothing more
than being able to focus in a way he had not previously done.

When we face temporal problems in our lives, it
can be easy to become overwhelmed and lose
hope. However, looking beyond those
problems, and intentionally choosing to
observe the greater reality, can inspire wonder
and awe in us. Consider the thing you pray
about most often. How have you observed it?

By recognizing the supernatural objective reality above and beyond our superficial subjective experiences, we can gain a greater perspective on our lives and challenges. We can find hope and comfort in the knowledge that God sees things from a divine perspective, and because of our union with Him, we can align our observations with His perspective. "Let this mind be in you which was also in Christ Jesus," Paul encouraged the Philippians.

Choose now to take control of where you focus and how you observe it. Begin to filter the external through the eternal before you let it become internal. Rise above the gutter clutter of life on a lower frequency and appropriate the focus of faith. A momentous decision that will position you to see your prayers answered is to observe life from the vantage point of the right hand of the Father because that is where you are seated at this very moment.

Chapter 5

Quantum Coherence and Abiding in Christ

Quantum coherence is a term used in quantum mechanics to describe the degree to which the properties of particles are correlated. When particles are in a state of coherence, they behave as a single system because their properties are interconnected and interdependent.

An illustration of coherence in everyday life could be a group of musicians playing together in a band. If each musician plays their own melody or rhythm, the result would be chaos and discord. However, if the musicians work together to create a cohesive sound, with each instrument complementing the others and playing in time, the result would be a beautiful and harmonious performance. In this example, the musicians work in a state of coherence, aligning their actions and efforts toward a common goal.

. . .

An example closer to how quantum energy works could be water waves on a pond. Imagine the water's surface is still until you throw a large rock into it. The rock hitting the water will cause a ripple or wave to extend outward from where it hit. Now imagine someone else immediately throws another large rock just a moment after yours hits the water. Their rock, too, will create a wave that moves outward.

Now you have two waves in the same pond. It's still one pond but finding expression through two waves. Each wave has a crest and a trough. The crest is the highest part of the wave, and the trough is the lowest. It's like when you're on a boat moving up and down through the waves.

Energy works the same way. Inside the quantum world, it exists in wave form (and particle form, too). When the peaks of two waves coincide, their wave functions combine to form a larger wave function. When they come together in this way, at the same phase, this results in what scientists call "constructive interference," where the height (amplitude) of the resulting wave function is increased by the combined "cooperation" of the two.

Think of the pond again. If the rocks are thrown, and the peak of one wave interacts with the trough of the other, they cancel each other, and the water will flatten out. This happens with energy, too. If the waves meet at the same phase, they gain momentum. However, if they meet when one is in peak phase and the other at a trough phase, the result is "destructive interference."

To simplify it, when the waves meet at the same phase, they work together, and the wave-particle is more likely to be found in a specific place (constructive interference). On the other hand, if the waves are out of sync, they cancel each other out, and the particle is less likely to be found in that place (destructive interference).

For example, if a surfer catches a wave formed by constructive interference, his goal to surf will be successful, and although he can't be sure exactly where he will end up on the beach, he knows the wave will carry him there. On the other hand, if two waves cancel each other out, there's nothing for him to ride, and he's going nowhere because of destructive interference.

ABIDING IN CHRIST AND CONSTRUCTIVE COHERENCE

Now, let's take this phenomenon of quantum coherence and use it as a framework for abiding in Christ. What does it mean to abide in Christ? The apparent meaning of the word applies to us all. As Paul told the crowd on Mars Hill, "In Him, we live and move and exist." Just as every ounce of water in the pond abides in the pond, so do we all abide in Christ in one sense of the word.

However, there is another way the word *abide* can be understood. It can be seen clearly through the lens of quantum coherence. This is where constructive and destructive coherence illustrates the point well. There is never a moment when you (the particle) are not in Christ (the pond), but how you function can be constructive or destructive to your success in the grace walk.

Jesus said, "Abide in me, and I in you. As the branch cannot bear fruit by itself unless it abides in the vine, neither can you unless you abide in me. I am the vine; you are the branches. Whoever abides in me and I in him, he it is that bears much fruit, for apart from me you can do nothing." (JOHN 15:4-5, ESV)

When He told His disciples "Abide in me, and I in you," there is a sense in which that was their fixed state of being and had nothing to do with their choice. The Bible clearly states, "It is by His doing that you are in Christ Jesus." (1 CORINTHIANS 1:30) That is an act of God. It's not something you constantly choose.

But Jesus spoke in that passage of something more than finding our existence in Him. He was talking about a way to function in faith. To abide in that sense of the word is to trust Him as our life source. It's what the Bible calls "walking in the Spirit." It's not a religious lifestyle but a righteous life rooted in our union with Christ. To abide in Christ is to reject the religious regiment we are often told we must follow and simply look to Him to animate our actions. It's not complicated. Religion makes it hard, but grace doesn't. In fact, in Matthew 11:30, Jesus called it "easy." It's legalism that complicates everything.

The instruction to abide in Christ is a spiritual application of constructive coherence. Remember, all the waves of water are in the same pond, whether constructive or destructive. Do you recognize the spiritual implication of this fact? The union both waves share with the whole is immutable, regardless of their behavior. We remember from the first chapter, 13th-century mystic Rumi said, "You are not a drop in the ocean. You are the entire ocean in a drop." That will never change. In the existential sense of the word, you always "abide" in Christ. Your union with Him is absolute and unchanging, regardless of your actions.

When destructive coherence happens in the pond, the peak of one wave meets the trough of another, and momentum is brought to a standstill when the waves stall out. In the quantum world, destructive coherence can significantly affect quantum systems. It can cause interference patterns to reduce in intensity or even disappear, and it can also affect the behavior of entangled particles. In quantum devices and systems, it can be a source of noise and interference that hinders performance. In simple terms, it can make a mess of things.

Rumi used a drop as a metaphor for your identity.
Let's shift our focus and consider how a
particle can also be a metaphor for who we are.
We are individual human particles of divine
energy finding our source inside the greater
field of energy, which is Christ. He is the
Divine Energy that fills the cosmos. The
Matrix is a Person named Jesus Christ. He is
not just a pond but is the Ocean. He's not just
a wave-particle inside a field. He's the whole
Field.

You are always in coherence (union) with Him; nothing can change that. Regardless of how waves behave, they are in union with the ocean and retain the properties of the ocean. The question is, "What is your phase in life? Are you behaving in constructive coherence or destructive coherence?" At any moment in time, you can function either way. To walk in the Spirit leads to constructive coherence. This means that our mindset is to trust Christ to animate our thoughts and actions. The other option is what the Bible calls "walking after the flesh," which means living an ego-driven lifestyle. It is to act out of phase with the divine flow of the River of Life within you. When we live out of phase, it is destructive to the flow of our lives. Walking after the flesh will cause us to "flatten out" and lose our forward momentum in Christ.

. . .

Romans 8:6 says, "For the mind set on the flesh is death, but the mind set on the Spirit is life and peace." The first leads to destructive coherence, but the latter to constructive coherence. Both are coherent in that they are still interconnected to Christ but don't produce the same outcome. Nothing can ever separate you from God, but your experience of life in Him can be affected by the influences around you.

In quantum mechanics, outside influences can disturb the coherence of a system, leading to destructive interference. This can happen when a system interacts with its environment, causing the loss of quantum information and coherence through a process called decoherence. For example, when a system is exposed to external influences such as noise or temperature changes, the quantum states of its constituent particles can become out of sync and lose their coherence. This can lead to the degradation of the system's performance and affect the ability to perform quantum computations or exhibit quantum phenomena.

In the same way, external influences in our lives can disrupt our internal coherence and alignment with the Spirit of Christ, leading us to stop trusting Him to animate our lives and allowing ourselves to be driven by an external force instead of the Internal Source who is Christ. When we interact with our environment in an unhealthy and unwise way, spiritual decoherence is the result. When that happens, there is no more accurate word to describe it than "destructive." What happens is that the flow of faith stalls, and we stop experiencing the momentum of the Spirit in our lives.

We are still in union with God but have interfered with our progress in a destructive way.

WALKING AFTER THE FLESH AND DESTRUCTIVE COHERENCE

The impact destructive coherence (walking after the flesh) has on our prayer life is entirely predictable. Many have thought that God doesn't answer their prayers because they have misbehaved and that the solution is to change what they're doing. They wrongly believe that there is some moral merit system that God uses to decide whether to answer our prayers or not. They think that, because that's what they've been programmed to believe by a legalistic understanding of prayer. As stated in the second chapter, legalism is the system of living in which we try to make spiritual progress or gain God's blessings based on what we do. It's about behavior, and whether it's quantum or spiritual coherence, behavior has nothing to do with it.

> This ill-advised understanding of prayer causes people to think they need to improve in some way if they want their prayers answered: Stop misbehaving. Do right. Change your actions to get God on your side and answer your prayer. It makes perfect sense to the person brainwashed by Bible-babble that is lightyears away from what the Scripture teaches and from what expresses the heart of the Father. "What have I done wrong? What do I need to

do that I'm not doing?" These are the
tormenting taunts to troubled minds who still
think answered prayers have anything to do
with a merit system that fuels a mindset based
on deserving to have prayers answered.
Answered prayer isn't a response to actions
but attitude.

Biblically speaking, "whoever is united with the Lord is one with
him in spirit." (1 CORINTHIANS 6:17) In 2 Peter 1, the Apostle
Peter describes how God chose you and then plainly says in verse
4, "He did it so you could share in his nature" (*New International
Readers Version*). You are eternally entangled in the divine nature.
Just as quantum particles share the same properties, whether there
is constructive or destructive coherence, nothing changes who you
are in Christ.

Remember the definition given for entanglement in the second
chapter: "Two particles become linked in such a way that the state
of one particle defines the state of the other particle." How could
you ever be far from God and need to get closer to Him? He
defines you. You are His genealogy. How you behave has nothing
to do with that.

If trying harder isn't the pathway toward answered
prayers, what is? Trusting Him. That's it –

nothing more and nothing less. Trust elevates
you to a peak where your mind perfectly
coincides with the mind of Jesus Christ. "Seek
those things which are above, where Christ is,"
we are encouraged in Scripture. The trough of
trying isn't where you meet the answers to
prayer.

God isn't motivated to answer prayer because we try harder. It's
not that He is hesitant to help us. On the contrary, He delights in
answering prayer. Psalm 149:4 says, "For the Lord takes pleasure in
his people." (ESV) He's not scrutinizing your actions, waiting for
you to get them right so He can answer.

Then why doesn't the answer come? It's because that's not how
God works. Prayer isn't manipulation because we do certain
things that convince Him to answer. Neither is it magic that
causes what we want to happen when we learn the right formula.
Instead, prayer is aligning your mind with the mind of Christ. At
that point, we experience constructive coherence and can ride the
wave into the manifestation we've prayed to receive.

Don't focus on trying to behave better, but instead, put your
attention on the goodness of God and open yourself to whatever
He wants to do in your situation. When you abandon yourself to
the flow of His faithfulness, you have met Him at the place where

miracles happen. You have moved into the phase of constructive coherence. Cast yourself into the current of Christ in total abandon, and you will not drown. Stop struggling to survive and rest in the realization that He will direct the details you have futilely fought to manage.

When we cast ourselves headlong into the bottomless ocean of God's love, we discover a place of rest and peace that surpasses all understanding. We can let go of our fears, anxieties, and worries about how things will turn out because we know that we are carried by the cooperative current of Christ's compassion. Where we end up may appear uncertain for now, but He guides the flow. Rest in the depth of His love, and the resulting constructive coherence, which is the work of the Spirit, will lead you to answers above and beyond anything you could ask or think.

CHAPTER 6

QUANTUM RESONANCE AND THE POWER OF FAITH

How did Jesus perform so many miracles during His earthly ministry? The disciples were often baffled by the things He did. For example, one day, Jesus fed a large crowd with only five loaves of bread and two fish. The people were amazed. As were the disciples. Later, after the crowd had dispersed, they asked Jesus, "What shall we do, that we may work the works of God?" It's a fair question and one we all would like to have answered.

Jesus pointed them to the heart of seeing miracles happen when He told them, "This is the work of God, that you believe in Him whom He sent." Not exactly the answer they were looking for, but one that is fundamental to seeing the miraculous manifest in our lives.

Let's be clear before we go any further in this
chapter. The starting place for any miraculous
answer to prayer is Jesus Christ. This
anchoring truth sets our approach apart from
many who embrace these quantum
phenomena. But on the other hand, it's not
only Christ-followers who have seen results
from a quantum approach. New Age
proponents sometimes see great results
through quantum phenomena. Name-it-and-
claim-it religious fanatics do, too. Even witch
doctors in tribal villages see results. How do I
suggest that Jesus Christ is the starting place
for miracles?

Think of it like this: God has set specific natural laws in place that
are absolute and universal in this world. They are absolute because
they never fail and are universal because they function everywhere.
For instance, the law of aerodynamics is one of those laws. It
always works the same in every part of the world.

Airplanes fly because of the law of aerodynamics. An airplane can
be used to carry Bibles or to smuggle drugs. The law works
regardless of how it's used by those who fly. God doesn't let the
plane fly for one and not the other. He has established this natural
law, which works regardless of who avails themselves of its
usefulness.

. . .

Why would God allow charlatans, imposters, and even Christ-deniers to be able to do miraculous things? It's because He doesn't insist on getting the credit for His goodness. There's a story in the Old Testament that illustrates this very well.

Hosea, a prophet in Israel, was given an unusual command from God: to marry a promiscuous woman named Gomer. Despite the societal taboos against such a marriage, Hosea obeyed and took Gomer as his wife. At first, their union was blessed with children, but soon Gomer began to stray from her husband and committed adultery with other men. Multiple men.

Despite her infidelity, Hosea continued to love Gomer and provide for her, even when she turned to prostitution. She was not aware of his faithfulness. Hosea 2:5 shows how wrong she was about how her needs were being met. She said, "'I will go after my lovers, who give me my bread and my water, my wool and my flax, my oil, and my drink." It wasn't her lovers who did those things. It was her husband, but she didn't know that. The amazing thing was that he was willing to meet her needs despite receiving no credit or recognition. In fact, she gave credit to the wrong source.

That's a beautiful picture of God. There are quantum laws that He has set in place, and, like the law of aerodynamics or any other natural law, they work consistently and for everyone. Let's be clear, though, that when we say "they work," we mean that the God who established them is the Source behind their work. Like Hosea, God is behind the benefits of the quantum life, even when He doesn't get the credit for it or if someone else does. As Jesus said in the Sermon on the Mount, He "sends rain on the righteous and the unrighteous."

> Don't be tempted to reject applying quantum realities to your prayers just because someone you know who is misguided has learned to use them. Some have said, "That sounds New Age," or "That sounds like the prosperity message those TV evangelists preach," or "That sounds like one of those Eastern religions." Don't make that kind of mistake. You don't refuse to fly because drug smugglers use airplanes, too. God is generous and gracious enough to allow His quantum laws to function even though they are sometimes abused. Instead of rejecting the quantum approach because others have misused it, how about redeeming this approach?

You are at the halfway point of reading this book, and it is important to again call your attention to the centrality of Christ in this approach. I don't want you to think I'm giving you a formula. What I'm doing is giving you a blueprint for expressing the faith that is within you. Let's give credit where credit is due. We can do some things that are effective, but this is a decidedly Christocentric method for how we live. Having affirmed that these quantum laws are effective because Christ is the Source, it's safe to embrace them as an expression of faith. It's not a linear formula but a living faith that empowers you to live out this quantum life. Let's consider the way resonance activated the miracles of Jesus.

QUANTUM RESONANCE AND WORDS

In every instance where Jesus performed a miracle in the Bible, His words were the catalyst for manifesting a supernatural result. Things changed when Jesus set His mind on an outcome and spoke to the situation. In the New Testament, there are numerous examples of Jesus speaking to situations and causing transformation. For instance, when He healed the paralyzed man, He spoke the words "Get up, take your mat, and go home," and the man was healed. (MARK 2:1-12) In another instance, Jesus spoke to the storm and the waves, calming the sea. (MARK 4:35-41) Then there was the time Jesus spoke to the man with the withered hand which was instantly restored. (MARK 3:1-5)

Jesus turned water into wine, multiplied food, restored a severed ear, raised the dead, cursed a tree and caused it to die, healed a man's son from a great distance, and other things that defy explanation from a strictly physical perspective. These things were metaphysical and were, in fact, quantum.

. . .

Quantum resonance refers to the organization of two or more quantum systems in a way that they vibrate in harmony. This can occur when the energy levels of the systems are close enough to allow for energy transfer between them. Pay close attention to that fact. It's about the transfer of energy from one to another. The miracles of Jesus happened when His energy transferred to the situation He addressed, and the situation then aligned itself with His intention.

The result of resonance is a state of coherence where the systems are entangled and behave in a coordinated manner. What happens is that one is transformed by the energy of the other as it begins to respond to that energy. This quantum explanation of how resonance works is central in the ministry of Jesus and will transform your prayers about situations you face.

When Jesus spoke to the wind and waves, His voice carried an energy that caused the natural elements to align with what He said. When He spoke to a sick person's body, that same energy evoked a response as their body came into resonance with His words and intention. What energy was it at work in the miracles He did? It was the energy of God. You could be tempted to look at the miracles of Jesus and say, "Well, yes, He did the miracles, but Jesus was God incarnate. It was a divine power that was operative in His life." You would be correct. It was divine energy working in and through Him, but here's the thing: You possess that same energy.

. . .

In 1 Corinthians 12:6, the Bible says, "There are different kinds of working, but in all of them and in everyone it is the same God at work." The word "working" in this verse is the Greek word *energeia* and means precisely what it looks like. In Colossians 1:29, Paul spoke of his ministry as "the energy (*energeia*) of Christ that so powerfully works in me."

> Quantum prayer rises above the anemic religious
> method of praying that many learned. In the
> evangelical background of my past, prayer
> wasn't dissimilar to a wish list that I presented
> to God. I would offer the list to Him and ask
> Him to graciously grant my desires. Then I
> would hope, sometimes trying to muster
> enough positive thinking that it could be
> called faith.

Don't get me wrong. God does answer us, but effective prayer is much more than Him taking pity on us when we bring our puny, pathetic prayers to Him like a beggar asking for a crumb of bread. Quantum prayer happens when we speak and seek answers based on recognizing the energy that "so powerfully works in me." The answer to your prayer resides within you in Christ, so the only thing left is for it to manifest in your experience.

. . .

Remember how we discussed that all answers already exist in superposition? Your prayers aren't trying to create an answer but facilitating that answer from the invisible into the visible. An illustration of a guitar may help clarify.

Imagine sitting on a stool holding an acoustic guitar in your hand. Sitting directly across from you is another person, who is also holding an acoustic guitar. The guitar in each of your hands has six strings for the notes E, A, D, G, B, and E. Whichever string is plucked produces that particular note.

Let the guitars become a metaphor to explain how answered prayers can work. Think of each string on the other person's guitar as a possible outcome in the situation you've prayed for God to resolve. In this example, there are six of them, and the guitar holds all of them. That one guitar simultaneously holds six possible outcomes. In the same way, all the possible outcomes for your life exist in superposition, inside the Kingdom of God.

What would you do if you wanted to hear a D note from the guitar the other person held? You could ask her to pluck that string, hoping she would respond to your request. That may or may not bring the result you wanted. You'd have to ask and then wait and see.

. . .

Or, there is another way. You could pluck the D string on the guitar you held. When a string on one guitar is plucked, it vibrates, producing sound waves traveling through the air. If another guitar is nearby with a string tuned to the same frequency as the first guitar's string, the sound waves can cause that string to vibrate as well, producing the same note.

> This example of resonance with sound waves can apply to your prayers. The universe holds every possible outcome (every string) for your life, in Christ. While the guitar mentioned holds six options, the number of possible alternatives the quantum world holds for your life is innumerable.

You can pray in the traditional way and ask that your prayer be answered, then wait and see. Or, you can exercise your faith proactively by how you think and speak about your situation. Quantum resonance is a reality that can move you from being passive to participating in seeing your prayers answered. Be conscious of how you talk about the situation you're praying to find an answer to.

D IS FOR "DONE"

Think again about the resonance between the D string being plucked on the guitar and how it affects the other guitar's string.

When we pray from a place of perceived lack, we're out of tune with "the divine frequency." God is a good, generous God who has no desire to hold back anything good from you. Psalm 84:11 says, "For the LORD God is a sun and shield; the LORD bestows favor and honor. No good thing does he withhold from those who walk uprightly." The bottleneck in seeing our prayers answered is often on our end, not God's.

If you're holding a guitar and you want the D string on the other guitar to resonate with yours, it's necessary to pluck the note you want to hear. You might say that you have to appropriate that note you want by acting in a specific way. Project the note you want to come back to you.

It's the same with prayer. If we want our prayer answered, it's important to appropriate the outcome by behaving in a way that facilitates its manifestation. How do we do that? One way is by cultivating a heart of gratitude that flows from recognizing that God has already provided everything we need, even when we have not seen it visibly. Philippians 4:6 says, "Do not be anxious about anything, but in every situation, by prayer and petition, with thanksgiving, present your requests to God." Note that thanksgiving is to be a pervasive part of prayer.

When thanksgiving accompanies prayer, we no longer are praying from a position of perceived lack but with an attitude of gratitude that "plucks" the string that resonates with the heart of God and causes an answer to manifest. Think of the D string as representing "Done!" Then pray with thanksgiving as if what you have asked is already done, because in the eternal realm, it *is* done!

This custom of the culture of the Kingdom of Kindness is effective and has even been proven by science. A study by researchers at the University of California found that people who practiced gratitude regularly experienced greater well-being, including better sleep, more positive emotions, and a stronger immune system. Another study published in the *Journal of Alternative and Complementary Medicine* found that people who kept a gratitude journal experienced fewer symptoms of illness and had better overall health than those who did not. Still another study, published in the *Journal of Personality and Social Psychology*, found that expressing gratitude toward a romantic partner increased feelings of connection and satisfaction in the relationship. The fact is that gratitude is a grace gateway. It leads us to the outcomes we've prayed for because it resonates with the goodness of God.

> Whatever area of your life you've been praying about, stop thinking of the situation as something you lack and begin to see the eternal reality that you lack nothing. Focus on an outcome where your prayer has been answered until you sense gratitude rising within you. Utilize thanksgiving as a faith response that appropriates the answer you

want in the same way one would pluck the D string on one guitar to evoke the same note from another.

When you align your mind and heart with the mind and heart of Christ, miracles are the only thing that can happen. It's like tuning a radio to the frequency of the station you want to receive. Switch to the FM (faith mentality) station in approaching praying.

When your prayers resonate with God's generous and loving nature, you become open to the many ways in which God works in your life. You can then approach Him with joy and expectancy, knowing He is faithful to answer. Determine now to be mindful of the many things you have to be grateful for, and may your heart overflow with thanksgiving until it resonates with the response your Father is eager to demonstrate in your life.

CHAPTER 7

QUANTUM SYNCHRONICITY AND DANCING WITH THE SPIRIT

A t the heart of the quantum world is a fantastic phenomenon where two systems dance in perfect harmony. They behave as a single entity even though each maintains its own individuality. Their entanglement is the mysterious cause of two acting in synch as one. In this shadowy sphere of science, the lines become blurry when we try to understand where one system ends and the other begins. Their union has defined their essence, so it becomes impossible to speak of one without referring to the other.

We have already learned that quantum entanglement describes the fusion of two systems existing as one. Quantum synchronization explains the function of those systems as the result of that union. In one experiment, the Bell test, results demonstrate quantum synchronization through "synchronized spins." To understand this phenomenon, imagine a set of particles, such as electrons or atoms, that are entangled. The particles are prepared in a specific quantum state and then spun in one direction or another. Their spins are then carefully measured.

When one particle's spin is measured and found to be "up," the spin of the other particle instantly aligns in the same direction, no matter how far apart they are. This synchronization occurs in a way that breaks classical principles of communication because of the way the particles seem to communicate faster than the speed of light. It appears supernatural because it defies natural laws as we understand them. They function identically, as if they are one, even though they are still distinct. It's a baffling mystery. They are two and yet are in union in a way that they function as one.

SPIRITUAL SYNCHRONICITY

This quantum phenomenon is a beautiful picture of the way the members of the Trinity behave among themselves. While oneness exists among the Father, Son, and Spirit, they function as one in a synchronized movement that could be compared to a dance. In my book, *Beyond an Angry God*, I described the historical understanding of this behavior among the members of the Godhead:

"The ancient Church Fathers used a particular Greek word to describe this special relationship. It is the word *perichoresis*. The word first appears in writing in the seventh century. It refers to what some have called a "community of being," in which each Person, while maintaining His distinctive identity, shares His very essence with the Others who share that same essence with Him. The word denotes a oneness that creates a unified movement of intimate relationship that has been compared to a dance."

"Look again at the word "perichoresis," coming from the words *peri* and *chorein*. *Peri* denotes a circle as in the word "perimeter." The word "choreography" finds its origin in *chorein*. Put the two together, and it's easy to see why a circle dance is a good metaphor for the loving, synchronized movement of the Father, Son, and Spirit. God isn't a somber, fixed Deity who sits frozen on a divine throne from where He scrutinizes and judges His creatures. He might better be described as a Divine Dancer who eternally celebrates love and life in the Divine Dance that is Himself." [1]

The modern word "synchronization" also derives from Greek roots with *syn* meaning "together" and *chronos* meaning "time." The Trinity moves together in time to the music of their loving connection.

. . .

It's hard to read the words of Jesus about His relationship with the Father without seeing quantum synchronicity at work. "I and my Father are one," He said, and added at another time, "I do only what I see my Father doing." The fusion of the Trinity is the basis of the function of each of them. Three in one act together in a sanctified synchronicity that perfectly expresses the essence of each in a beautifully unified way that could be understood as a divine dance.

The thrilling facet of your authentic identity is that you, too, are a participant in this supernatural phenomenon. You don't stand apart from God but exist in Christ and, as such, are in union with the Trinity within whom all things exist. Physicist John Wheeler argued that we are not just bystanders on a cosmic stage but are shapers and creators living in "a participatory universe." Think of this "participatory universe" as scientific language describing the Kingdom of God and the stage as a ballroom floor where we join in the dance of the Trinity. The *evangelion* (gospel) of the New Testament is the good news that we have been included in the divine circle dance and are invited to knowingly and joyfully participate in the Spirit of Synchronicity who mediates the life of Divinity in and through our humanity.

Quantum synchronicity is the way to practice the biblical injunction to "walk in the Spirit." In the language of the church, it is to recognize our union with God and to allow His Spirit to express the supernatural life of Christ through the superficial lifestyle of our conduct. Sometimes church culture frames the idea of walking in the Spirit as a sort of religious regiment identified by a churchy talk and walk, but that is nothing more than a feeble attempt to imitate the real thing.

> Jesus Christ was a man, filled with the Spirit, and rather than fitting in with the religious crowd of His day, He offended them. On one occasion, He bluntly said to them, "But to what shall I compare this generation? It is like children sitting in the marketplaces and calling to their playmates, 'We played the flute for you, and you did not dance; we sang a dirge, and you did not mourn.'" (MATTHEW 11:16-17, ESV) He refused to conform to their expectations of what a good religious person should look like.

Perhaps the most significant impediment today to an authentic, Spirit-led lifestyle is the false notion so many Christ-followers have in thinking that they should be religious when the only thing they need to do is be real. Don't act spiritual. You *are* spiritual, so just be yourself. It may not be enough to satisfy the religious people who might judge you, but it's more than enough for God. Just be you.

Religion focuses on "getting it right," whether the
rightness is applied to belief or behavior. An
authentic grace walk is a lifestyle that rests in
the realization that we have nothing to prove
but are free to go with the flow of the faith
that fills us. Quantum synchronicity in our
spiritual walk is nothing other than moving in
synch with the indwelling Spirit without fear
that we might get it wrong.

JUST DANCE

I will never forget the time when I learned to dance. I had been
married for almost twenty years, and my wife and I went on our
first cruise with another couple. On the first night aboard the ship,
we had eaten dinner and were sitting together when a band began
to play, and singers began to perform. People soon moved from
their seats onto the main dance floor and began to dance together.

My wife looked at me and said, "Let's dance." There was one
problem with her request: I didn't know how to dance. She had
grown up dancing, but I grew up in a religious home where those
sorts of things weren't allowed, so I'd never learned how.

"You know I can't dance," I answered her.

.   .   .

"Please tell me we aren't going to spend the week on this ship and not be able to dance at all," she responded.

I was conflicted. On the one hand, I loved my wife and wanted to dance for her sake, but on the other, I didn't know how to dance. I told her again, "But I don't know how to dance."

"I'll teach you. It's easy," she said.

"Okay, let's wait for a good song," I answered.

Shortly, a familiar song began to play, and she said, "That's a good one. Let's go."

Reluctantly, I walked to the dance floor with her. "Just listen to the beat," she said. "One, two, one-two-three. One, two, one-two-three."

I began to count the beat in my mind, held her close, and began to move. "One, two, one-two-three. One, two, one-two-three," I repeated in my head as I stared at my feet.

"Do you hear the rhythm?" she asked. "It's a cha-cha beat."

. . .

"Stop talking to me. Now I've lost count," I answered in frustration.

Then she lovingly said, "Steve. Stop watching your feet. Look at me and relax."

So I did. I looked into the face of the only woman I'd ever loved . . . the face of the woman I had begun to date at sixteen years old and then married three years later . . . the face that had laughed and cried with me for decades. And then, it happened. Caught up in the moment of dancing with the woman I loved, I began to feel the rhythm of the music. I lost consciousness of whether or not I was in step with the beat. I became captured by the moment, the music, and the intimacy shared with my lover, and I danced. I never again worried about how I performed on the dance floor. I just danced.

That's synchronicity. Two moving together as one. That is the relationship you have with God. In The Message, Jesus said, "Walk with me and work with me—watch how I do it. Learn the unforced rhythms of grace. I won't lay anything heavy or ill-fitting on you. Keep company with me, and you'll learn to live freely and lightly." (MATTHEW 11:29-30)

. . .

Synchronicity is the "unforced rhythm" of moving in step with the Spirit in our daily lives. Prayer is nothing less than a sacred movement that happens when we align ourselves with the guidance of the Spirit and our desires harmonize with God's will for us. As we move in rhythm with His plan, the sanctified synchronicity of our lives takes us to a higher level as we function from the unction of being entangled with the One who wrote the beautiful melody which is our life. How could our prayers possibly not be answered when we live that way?

As dance partners lean into each other and surrender to the music, something beautiful happens. To allow the Spirit to lead you is to participate in the unfolding of the divine plan and power that guides your life. You may be tempted to try to function on your own if the sound of the music of your circumstances seems to be in a minor key, but fear not. Christ, the Composer, and the Spirit within you are moving in perfect union to demonstrate the dance of grace in and through you. Just yield yourself and follow the moves of the Spirit.

STOP FOCUSING ON THE RIGHT STEPS

When I was preoccupied with my steps on the dance floor, I was deaf to the music and blind to the beauty of my partner. It was when I put my focus on her and was fully present to her love that I lost the fear of missteps, began to hear the melody, and found myself being absorbed into the intimacy of the moment. I never took a dance lesson. I stopped counting the beats. I went with the flow and danced. Was I a good dancer? What does it matter? I was moving to the music and discarded the whole construct of performance. I abandoned myself to the moment, the music, and my Melanie.

> Quantum prayer works that way. It happens when you stop focusing on steps and follow the Spirit in a synchronized sway of loving submission. Resist the urge to lead the dance and abandon the notion that you can write the song of your situation better than God can do it.

Embrace being immersed in the intricate steps and movements of life, guided by the Musician who orchestrates your journey. Just as a dancer engages with various movements, spins, and gestures, you will encounter a range of experiences, emotions, and challenges throughout your life. We all sway between joy and sorrow, triumph and defeat, love and heartache. The rhythm of life carries us forward, urging us to embrace each beat and step with intention and purpose. We learn to move with the ebb and flow, gracefully adapting to the changing cadence of circumstances.

In the sacred dance of life, we learn the art of surrender and trust, allowing the divine music to guide our every move. We discover that the steps we take, our leaps of faith, and the twirls of joy we experience are all part of a grand choreography orchestrated by a loving Composer. Embrace the dance, finding meaning, purpose, and connection as you move through life in synch with the unforced rhythms of grace. As you practice this, you will experience the Spirit dancing you into the answer to your prayers.

CHAPTER 8

QUANTUM UNCERTAINTY AND ADVENTURE

In the world of quantum physics, there exists an inherently unpredictable element known as the principle of quantum uncertainty, formulated by Werner Heisenberg, a German theoretical physicist and one of the key pioneers of quantum mechanics. His work has had profound implications on physics and philosophy, earning him the Nobel Prize in Physics in 1932. Thankfully, quantum uncertainty can even teach us about prayer.

This fundamental concept of the uncertainty principle states that it is impossible to simultaneously measure a particle's exact position and momentum with absolute certainty. The more precisely one property is measured, the less precisely the other can be known. At first glance, this might seem far removed from our everyday lives and even further from the subject of prayer. Bu this principle, existing at the heart of the physical universe, offers a profound metaphor for our relationship to matters of prayer. Just as quantum particles exist in a state of flux and potentiality, so, too, do we navigate through life in what we often experience as a state of "uncertainty," relying on faith in God rather than our own ability to foresee the future. In the same way that a particle's position and momentum can't be precisely known, we often can't see both the details of our immediate circumstances and the bigger picture of God's plan simultaneously.

The problem most of us have when we pray about the things that concern us is that we are anxious to know the details of how our situation might be resolved. As a result, our brains often go into hyperdrive trying to figure out every option we might have. That alone frustrates us, because, as we've already learned, every possibility exists in superposition. It's impossible to know which of those innumerable outcomes will be the precise one to manifest in our experience. Then add to that the urge to know when the circumstance will change, and it's enough to cause anyone to be restless instead of being in a state of peace.

The old-school science we were all taught infiltrated the viewpoint about prayer many people have. Quantum mechanics dismantles the mindset that holds to doing specific things to guarantee predictable answers. We don't control God or our world. We have influence but not domination over exact outcomes. We cooperate with the culture of the Kingdom but are usually ignorant of how God will answer our prayers. The Apostle Paul said, "For we live by faith, not by sight." (2 CORINTHIANS 5:7, NIV) T.S. Elliot affirmed the same when he wrote, "In order to arrive at what you do not know, you must go by a way which is the way of ignorance." [1]

To figure out the what and when of seeing your prayer answered defies the need for faith. In this quantum landscape, particles exist in a state of superposition, embodying every possibility. They only have definite positions of speed once measured. It is a world where the traditional deterministic laws yield to the probabilistic rules of quantum mechanics.

This characteristic of the nature of reality fundamentally changed the scientific understanding of how the world works. In the old Newtonian world of predictability, we believed that if we knew the current state of a system and the laws that govern its behavior, we could predict its future state with certainty. Quantum discoveries have overturned that perspective by showing that, at its smallest scales, the future isn't set in stone, but is probabilistic. The more accurately we know a particle's position, the less sure we can become of its velocity and vice versa. This means our ability to predict and control the future is fundamentally limited.

Although the Newtonian, mechanistic approach to science is applicable on a macroscopic level, it fails us at the microscopic level. We can still accurately predict the stars' location, and the timing of the sunrise and sunset, but we don't know precisely how subatomic particles will behave, because it's a different world altogether.

> The invisible world of the Kingdom of God isn't something that we can control using religious formulas. We want to figure it all out to control it, but it doesn't work that way. God once told the prophet, "For my thoughts are not your thoughts, neither are your ways my ways," declares the Lord. "As the heavens are higher than the earth, so are my ways higher than your ways and my thoughts than your thoughts." (ISAIAH 55:8-9)

Legalistic religion insists on specific outcomes that we dictate. We've sometimes been told that we can see what we want to happen right down to the minute details if we meet the criteria imposed on us. What those criteria are depends on the religious sect that instructs us. However, the reality is that we can't control outcomes. Prayer isn't a magic genie. Although the phenomena discussed in the previous chapters are all valid, none of these guarantee an exact outcome. Faith in a loving God, combined with confidence in a grace-filled result, moves us toward the perfect answer to our prayer without knowing the specifics of that answer.

. . .

Heisenberg's uncertainty principle causes us to rethink our notions of reality and possibility and encourages us to embrace uncertainty as an integral facet of our existence. Faith is an adventure of trust and hope that doesn't include detailed certitude and predictable outcomes but confidence in God's constant presence and guidance in our lives. Just as scientists can't simultaneously know a particle's location and velocity, neither can we know everything about how God will answer our prayer, but we can know that the prayer will be answered. The elements of when and how are outside our control, but you can rest assured that inside the Kingdom of Kindness, the answer already exists and will manifest at the precise time and exact way that is best.

EMBRACING MYSTERY

This element of uncertainty that exists in our experience of Ultimate Reality is what many in the Judeo-Christian tradition have called "mystery." The infinite ways of God exceed our finite ability to understand more than we can imagine. Uncertainty is unavoidable because we don't know everything. What we do know is that God is good at every moment, so that's what we lean into when we pray about our circumstances.

Mystery is a central component of life, an essential spice that makes the journey of our lives flavorful. It's in the unknown that creativity thrives, and our potential unfolds. We sometimes approach the mysterious or the unfamiliar with apprehension or fear, but it's in those very spaces of uncertainty that life expands and miracles occur. Instead of fearing the unknown, we should greet it with curiosity and openness. A positive mindset transforms the mystery from a source of fear into a sphere of faith, turning shadows into stepping stones that lead toward growth and discovery of divine plans for our lives that we wouldn't know otherwise.

In the embrace of mystery, some of the most beautiful chapters of our lives often get written. Think about times in your life when the future was uncertain, but a beautiful picture emerged as time passed. As you face uncertain times, consciously activate your faith. Remind yourself that God is God and God is good. You have a Friend who sticks closer than a brother and Who will walk with you through the darkness until you come out on the other side.

Don't focus on problems but on the Person who understands every detail of the situation and already holds the outcome. You may be looking for solutions, but God may be working in your situation in a beautiful and beneficial way that a quick fix would short-circuit. Stand still in the darkness, and wait to hear His voice. This is a holy moment. Don't waste it. Allow uncertainty to guide you into a more profound connection with God. When you don't know how to work out the details of the external, press into the depths of the eternal.

French philosopher Gabriel Marcel, one of the most influential thinkers of the 20th century, distinguishes between "problems" and "mysteries" by explaining that we can solve problems but can only contemplate mysteries. He made the case that theology must embrace the "mysterious" at its core while science focuses on problem-solving. [2] There is a time to crack codes and solve the problem, but sometimes the greater opportunity is to contemplate Christ and see the Person who may well have brought you into the darkness for a time to take you away from the distractions that would interfere with a clear view of His presence. Don't miss the gifts of grace that can only be delivered in the dark by becoming frantic about moving past it.

Keep your eyes on the One who holds all the answers in His hands, and don't get bogged down in trying to solve the problem. Instead, envision a grace-filled outcome and rest in the unknown with confidence that He is lovingly attending to you and your situation even when you can't see how. When there is something you're supposed to do, He will tell you. When you don't know what to do, don't be afraid but embrace the mystery of it all. It can feel scary to realize you aren't in control, but it can also feel exciting. Soren Kierkegaard said, "To dare is to lose one's footing momentarily. Not to dare is to lose oneself." [3] So go ahead, throw yourself into Divine Darkness. You can do that by faith.

GOD RESIDES INSIDE THE UNKNOWN

In the biblical account of Exodus 20, Moses leads the Israelites out of Egypt after God performs a series of miraculous plagues and parts the Red Sea. They find themselves in the wilderness, at the foot of Mount Sinai, where the presence of God descends upon the mountain, enveloping it in smoke and fire. Moses climbs the mountain and leaves the Israelites behind at the base. The people watch as he ventures into the darkness, and it is during this time that Moses receives the Ten Commandments from God.

The scene is described in Exodus 20:18-21:

> "Now all the people witnessed the thunderings, the lightning flashes, the sound of the trumpet, and the mountain smoking, and when the people saw it, they trembled and stood afar off. Then they said to Moses, 'You speak with us, and we will hear; but let not God speak with us, lest we die.'
>
> And Moses said to the people, 'Do not fear; for God has come to test you, and that His fear may be before you, so that you may not sin.' So the people stood afar off, but Moses drew near the thick darkness where God was."
> (NKJV)

Note the difference between Moses and the rest. They stood in fear in the face of uncertainty. Moses drew near the thick darkness. His example stands as a teacher to us all. When you can't see what's ahead, embrace the uncertainty. Don't run from it. Enter it.

. . .

The Scripture gives the reason we can embrace the darkness in no uncertain terms. "Moses drew near the thick darkness *where God was.*" It's our natural tendency to assume that bad things are inside the darkness, but that's not what the Bible says. It is in the darkness that we encounter God.

The Copenhagen interpretation of quantum science suggests that every outcome already exists in superposition and that it's an observation that influences which one manifests. The Bible says that all things are possible with God. Therefore, anything can happen, not just the unwanted things.

When you stand in the face of uncertainty, you find yourself in an exhilarating position. Better things can come to you than you could conceive in your wildest dreams. Uncertainty is the greatest ground of grace upon which you will ever stand. So don't shirk back but "draw near the thick darkness," because that's where the miracles happen.

Embrace the unknown. Let the veils of uncertainty be the canvas upon which your courage paints. It's in the heart of the "thick darkness" that we truly find ourselves, our potential, and our faith. It's not a void; it's an arena of endless possibilities, a birthing place of miracles and wonders. What may seem opaque and impenetrable is actually the womb of creation, where the extraordinary happens, where we are shaped and remolded, honed, and polished in the hands of God by life's mysterious ways. Boldly enter the unknown! Lean into the shadows with an open heart, and let the unexpected guide you. For it's in the mysterious darkness that the stars of miracles twinkle, and it's by drawing near to it that we can reach out and touch them.

CHAPTER 9

QUANTUM TUNNELING AND ADVERSITY

I magine you are staring at a fifteen-foot brick wall stretching as far as you can see in both directions. You want to get to the other side, but the wall is too high to climb and reaches too far to go around. You take a running start, fling yourself toward the wall with all your might, and slam right into the hard bricks. As you pick yourself up and rub your bruised shoulder, it becomes clear that getting to the other side is impossible. Or is it?

What if you could walk through the wall to the other side? Defying all logic, you could find yourself there without breaking down the wall, climbing over it, or going around it. Sound impossible? It's not.

John 20:19-20 records a time when Jesus did it:

"So when it was evening on that day, the first day
of the week, and when the doors were shut
where the disciples were, for fear of the Jews,
Jesus came and stood in their midst and said to
them, 'Peace be with you.' And when He had
said this, He showed them both His hands and
His side. The disciples then rejoiced when
they saw the Lord."

"The doors were shut" when they looked and saw Jesus in the
room with them. Can you imagine such a thing? The disciples
must have been shocked at such a miraculous event, and
understandably so. The fantastic thing we now know is that His
ability to pass through the shut doors and come into the room has
a scientific grounding in the field of quantum physics. As mind-
bending as it sounds, quantum tunneling allows solid particles to
pass through barriers they shouldn't be able to cross. Is it science,
or is it a miracle? Yes, it's both!

Remember that scientific realities don't oppose the world of
miracles. Instead, they open the world of miracles to us!
Augustine understood this when he wrote, "Miracles are not
contrary to nature, but only contrary to what we know of nature.
For we call those things natural, which we are used to, being
ignorant of the true nature of things." [1]

. . .

I'm not going to try to teach you about walking through literal walls in this chapter, even though it's not as far-fetched an idea as we once thought. Understanding how quantum tunneling is already being used in our modern world can open our minds to things that have been unthinkable until now. Today, research has been done with quantum tunneling microscopes, showing how particles pass through solid barriers. [2] It has also been used in electronics with tunnel diodes for the purpose of facilitating fast electronic switching. [3] Researchers have learned that it even happens inside our bodies when enzymes speed up chemical reactions. [4] Quantum tunneling is a weird phenomenon to our logical minds, but modern science has proven it is an indisputable reality.

This fantastic scientific feat is an excellent metaphor for life. Not only did Jesus pass through the shut doors of the upper room, but He did something even greater than that. He passed through the barriers of death and the grave. Remember that He said we would do the things He did and, in fact, even greater things. (SEE JOHN 14:12) If death isn't insurmountable to any of us, that fact gives us a powerful insight into navigating our way through the obstacles we face in life. If passing through death is possible, nothing is insurmountable.

DEAD ENDS ARE NOT DEAD ENDS

In our daily lives, we all run up against barriers that seem impenetrable. It might be a scary medical diagnosis that dumps us into despair. A failed relationship can make us feel walled off from love. Shattered dreams can shut down our sense of purpose. So much can happen in life that leaves us feeling there's no way forward, no hope of getting to the other side. It's easy sometimes to feel like we've reached a dead end and there's no way out.

When we are tempted to look at our circumstances and conclude that we're facing an impossible situation, it's important to remember that God has an excellent track record when it comes to impossible situations. Anything can happen inside the Kingdom of God, and when we open our minds to see that we live in a "matrix of miracles," we put ourselves in a posture to see unthinkable things happen for our benefit.

In the close-ended world of cause and effect, outcomes rely on linear progression, but inside the quantum world of God's Kingdom, ordinary rules are suspended so that we move through obstacles in life in ways that often defy explanation. Answers can seem to come out of nowhere.

Our tendency when we face adversity in life is to immediately fall into an analytical mindset that tries to figure out what to do to remedy the problem. There are times in life when there's simply nothing left for us to do outwardly. In those moments, we stand at the portal to the supernatural, whether we know it or not.

What adverse challenges are you facing now? Open your mind. Look beyond the superficial, temporal details and gaze into the supernatural, transcendent domain where the laws of life you have come to know are turned on their heads. If we claim to be people of faith, let's choose to act in faith even when it seems ridiculous.

When Moses led Israel out of Egypt, they soon found themselves standing at the Red Sea with no hope of surviving their desperate situation. Pharoah's army was closing in on them from the rear, and the vast Red Sea was directly in front of them. Understandably, the people were in complete panic mode. Exodus 14:10-12 describes their state of mind:

> "As Pharaoh approached, the Israelites looked up,
> and the Egyptians were marching after them.
> They were terrified and cried out to the Lord.
> They said to Moses, 'Was it because there were
> no graves in Egypt that you brought us to the
> desert to die? What have you done to us by
> bringing us out of Egypt? Didn't we say to
> you in Egypt, "Leave us alone; let us serve the
> Egyptians"? It would have been better for us
> to serve the Egyptians than to die in the
> desert!'"

. . .

After pouring his own anxious fears out to God, Moses gave the people instructions that would open the way for an answer to manifest. Verses 13-14 say,

> "And Moses said unto the people, 'Fear ye not,
> stand still, and see the salvation of the LORD,
> which he will shew to you today: for the
> Egyptians whom ye have seen today, ye shall
> see them again no more forever. The LORD
> shall fight for you, and ye shall hold your
> peace.'"

In the face of imminent danger and overwhelming fear, Moses gave instructions that made no sense in the world of ordinary logic. "Stand still." At a moment when panic had gripped the people, leading them to consider retreating or even regretting their escape from Egypt, Moses told them to stop freaking out and just to be still. By doing that, he shifts their focus from linear logic to a supernatural strategy. In this context, standing still isn't a passive act but a form of active faith. It is a physical manifestation of trust in God, allowing the people to create the mental and emotional space for a miracle to occur. Without their frantic scrambling, they witnessed the "salvation of the Lord" as the Red Sea parted to provide them a path to freedom. They were about to pass through the obstacle but needed to "get their minds right" before that could happen.

HOW WE THINK MAKES ALL THE DIFFERENCE

That's often the case for us when we face threatening situations. If we want to pass through an insurmountable problem, changing how we think is often necessary. The catalyst for a miracle usually starts in our minds.

Since Moses gave these instructions to the people of Israel, science has come along and explained the practical power inherent to the divine direction Moses spoke millennia ago. We now are able to understand not only that God continues to tell us to be still and not worry but also to know why we're told that and how it works.

The beta brainwave state, ranging from 13 to 30 Hz, is the most common waking state of the brain. It is associated with active thinking, problem-solving, and concentration. When you're engaged in mental activities, speaking, or making quick decisions, your brain is usually in a beta state. That's where you are in problem-solving mode.

While that function is vital to us in daily life, we sometimes need a mental shift to get answers. Staying in the beta phase when we can't solve problems can be draining and lead to stress and anxiety.

The Israelites were clearly in beta-state overdrive when Moses came back with instructions from God to stand still.

Alpha brainwaves, which oscillate between 8 and 13 Hz, are often associated with a state of relaxed alertness, creativity, and a bridge to the subconscious mind. Unlike the high-frequency beta waves that dominate during periods of analytical thinking and stress, alpha waves allow the mind to enter a calmer, more receptive state. This shift can enable us to make unique connections and access insights that often escape us in a beta state. In the context of a lifestyle of grace, the alpha state can be particularly transformative by moving us from trusting logical facts to a living faith that allows for miracles. It takes us from the driven state of mind to a receptive posture.

During stressful times, when the mind is racing in beta, it can be challenging to feel connected to God or to trust that He can change things for us. When we shift to the alpha state, we find it easier to surrender control and trust Him. This relaxed yet focused state positions us to miraculously move through our crisis just as Israel finally passed through the Red Sea on dry land. It was an outcome that could never have happened by their beta state problem-solving efforts.

Numerous studies have used EEG, brain imaging, hormones, and behavioral tests to demonstrate the benefits of transitioning from active beta states to more relaxed and inwardly focused alpha states. There are also many testimonials from people who report feeling a deep connection to God while in the alpha state. Alpha waves quiet the hyperactive mind, enhance intuition, and heighten the senses in a way many have described as "spiritual," even if they don't consider themselves religious.

Faith taps into a higher dimension where moving through closed doors or seeing a sea of water stand up to make a way to pass through is not only impossible but is the culture of that Kingdom. Quantum tunneling is a proven phenomenon in the physical realm, but it's even more exciting to recognize that it points toward a greater reality. It points to a spiritual world where we can move through agonizing adversity in a way that cannot happen if we use only the tools of human capability.

PROBLEMS CAN BECOME PORTALS

With God, all things are possible. We open up quantum possibilities beyond our wildest imagination by looking through the external into the eternal. Answers can come. Peace can prevail in our thoughts and feelings even when external evidence could evoke fear and panic. No barrier is too great to traverse when we "stand still and see the salvation of the Lord." Shut doors are nothing to the One who can pass through them and take us with Him.

No adversity is too big for the One who animates
your life when you drop out of the ego-driven

world, still your turbulent thoughts, and look
past the daunting walls and deep waters that
seem to block your way. Take hold of the
quantum realities available inside God's
Kingdom. Look beyond earthly problems and
see eternal possibilities.

In the amazing world of quantum mechanics, quantum tunneling
defies the conventional boundaries of physics. What looks like a
mystical movement of particles accomplishes what seems
impossible. It's a good metaphor that resonates far beyond the
realm of science. As captivating as it is, quantum tunneling
mirrors a truth that transcends physical laws, calling us to consider
the profound parallels it shares with our faith.

Consider the particles that, against all odds, move through barriers
that once appeared impenetrable. They don't quit in the face of
adversity but press onward. In the same vein, Christ's life instills in
us a spirit of perseverance—an unyielding determination to rise
above challenges and press on toward our divine calling. Just as
particles harness their innate potential, so do we possess an
inherent strength expressed by Christ's life within us.

You are a vessel of divine energy in union with Christ's miraculous
power. The adversity that would block you is an opportunity to
see Christ do what He does—move you ahead when it looks

impossible. Like particles that surge forward, guided by a force beyond comprehension, you, too, are guided by an unwavering faith that transcends the barriers of doubt.

Although we've considered quantum tunneling a metaphor, the life of Christ within you is not merely a metaphor—it is an invincible truth, a reminder that you are equipped to overcome, flourish, and leave a trail of inspiration in your wake.

It's time to move forward. You are more than a conqueror through Him who lives within you. The obstacles may be towering, the path uncertain, but you are equipped with Divine Life that turns the impossible into the inevitable—a testament to the boundless grace that propels you through the impossible to the Him-possible.

CHAPTER 10

QUANTUM LEAPS AND SPIRITUAL GROWTH

In physics, a quantum leap is a sudden, discontinuous change in the state of a physical system. It happens when an electron instantly jumps from one energy level to another instead of happening gradually. Think of driving down the interstate and going from mile marker 100 to mile marker 150 without moving past the markers in between. That's the sort of thing that happens in a quantum leap. Quantum leaps make no sense in classical physics and are often described as seemingly impossible.

In 1914, James Franck and Gustav Hertz conducted an experiment that proved the veracity of quantum leaps and how strange they are. The experiment involved firing electrons through a tube filled with mercury vapor. As the electrons moved through the tube, they would collide with mercury atoms. If an electron had enough energy, it would "excite" a mercury atom, instantly causing one of its electrons to jump to a higher energy level. The key finding was that this energy transfer only happened at specific energy levels. In other words, the electron could only "jump" if it had a precise amount of energy, and when that happened, it went from one energy level to another instantly. It might be compared to putting a pot of water on the stove to boil and having it go from cold to boiling immediately instead of gradually. This is known as a "quantum leap." Their experiment was significant enough that Franck and Hertz won the Nobel Prize for their findings. [1]

In the fantastic journey that is your life, there is a Bridge that connects you to the potential for giant strides like you have never imagined. Open your mind and allow the final chapter of this book to be your springboard into a new way of living that is as different from a close-ended religious lifestyle to a genuinely supernatural lifestyle as the linear world of scientific materialism is to quantum physics. Quantum leaps don't just happen in labs. They can occur in life to those who understand the Kingdom of God and how to live in it. You can miraculously see your prayer answered in an instant as your faith rises to a new level because of the influence of Christ's indwelling life.

The lifestyle most believers in Christ have known is religious, regulated, and restrictive. Legalistic religion has reduced supernatural potential to superficial plans intended to move us forward one step at a time. It has told us that to have our prayers answered requires moving through certain stages based on actions we take in the right direction. What those paces are will depend on what a certain denomination may have taught us. It may include contrition and confession, praise and worship, repentance and rededication, partaking of the sacraments, memorizing the scriptures, prayer and fasting, or countless other things squarely situated in the world of predictable cause and effect.

That is a mechanistic approach to life, but what if there is another way? A miraculous way to advance that isn't grounded in grit but guided by grace? What if, just as quantum physics transcends the classical physics of old-school science, there is a higher and better way to pray than the old-school religious way you were taught in church?

A quantum leap happens in the world of physics when a precise energy level affects a particle in a way that causes something "magical" to happen by instantly transforming it. There is an Energy that can do the same in your prayer life. The Apostle Paul knew this and prayed for the Ephesians that they would have "the eyes of [their] hearts enlightened, that [they] may know what is the hope to which he has called [them], what are the riches of his glorious inheritance in the saints, and what is the immeasurable greatness of his power toward [those] who believe, according to the working of his great might." (EPHESIANS 1:18-19 ESV)

According to this text, knowing the immeasurable greatness of divine power depends on "the working of His great might." When Paul used the word "working" to describe what divine might facilitates, he chose the Greek word *energeian*. The word was introduced in chapter six. You can look at that word and see the English equivalent without much of a challenge. It's the word often translated as "energy."

Quantum prayer happens when we stop thinking that our prayers are answered when we do the right thing and start believing that answered prayer results from His acting upon us and our circumstances simply because of grace. Are we passive in the process? No, of course not. This book has provided practical ways to cooperate with the working of God in our lives to answer our prayers, but we must never forget that "it is God who works in [us], both to will and to work for his good pleasure." (PHILIPPIANS 2:13, ESV)

The answer to your prayers can come gradually, but it doesn't have to happen that way. God's method for acting in our lives and circumstances is often sudden. Answers to problems can come instantaneously. What science calls a quantum leap is sometimes called "an epiphany, revelation, or rhema" in the vocabulary of faith. God can answer you in a moment. The answer you receive may not eliminate the problem, but equips you to face it. Remember that a quantum leap happens when there is an instantaneous jump from one energy level to another. This is what sometimes happens when we pray. We want God to work in our situation when he aims to work in us.

WAIT ON IT

The book of Habakkuk is one of the twelve minor prophets in the Old Testament and is situated in a period of great uncertainty and distress for the kingdom of Judah, one of the two ancient Israelite kingdoms. The Babylonian Empire was rising in power and would eventually conquer Judah in 586 BCE, leading to the destruction of the First Temple in Jerusalem and the beginning of the Babylonian Exile.

After being given the horrifying news about the trials that lay ahead for him and his fellow citizens, the Bible describes the contrast between Habakkuk's feelings and his faith this way:

> "I heard, and my heart pounded,
> my lips quivered at the sound;
> decay crept into my bones,
> and my legs trembled.
> Yet I will wait patiently for the day of calamity
> to come on the nation invading us.
> Though the fig tree does not bud
> and there are no grapes on the vines,
> though the olive crop fails
> and the fields produce no food,
> though there are no sheep in the pen
> and no cattle in the stalls,
> yet I will rejoice in the Lord,
> I will be joyful in God my Savior.

The Sovereign Lord is my strength;
he makes my feet like the feet of a deer;
he enables me to tread on the heights."
(HABAKKUK 3:16-19, NIV)

Sometimes, God doesn't take the problem away from us. He does something even more impressive. He lifts us inside the situation and energizes us to act in a way that defies logic. He lifts us to a higher level, energizing us with His indwelling life to see beyond our "day of calamity" and to experience His strength while we are still in our trial. When everything in the external world is disastrous, He enables us to rise above it and "to tread on the heights" while we wait.

The quantum principles discussed in this book aren't theoretical. They aren't magic. They are proven. There are times in life when, instead of taking us out of our problems, He makes us aware that He is with us in the trial. If the solution to your problem has yet to come, wait for it. In the meantime, God may be working in your life in a more helpful way than if He were to instantly take away the challenge you face. You are being elevated to a new level, where divine energy will sustain you and release you from the struggle of trying to manage it yourself.

Entrust yourself to the One who spoke everything into existence, and be assured that when your trouble doesn't stop, He is with you in it. As hard as it can be to accept, sometimes the answer is to wait. The sentiment of waiting on God for deliverance is a recurring theme in the book of Habakkuk, such as the text in chapter two, verses one through three:

"I will stand at my watch
and station myself on the ramparts;
I will look to see what he will say to me
and what answer I am to give to this complaint.
Then the Lord replied:
'Write down the revelation
and make it plain on tablets
so that a herald may run with it.
For the revelation awaits an appointed time;
it speaks of the end
and will not prove false.
Though it linger, wait for it;
it will certainly come and will not delay.'"

Wait. That may be the most significant expression of faith you can demonstrate at the moment. Show yourself grace if all you're doing is waiting for things to change while keeping your focus on Christ. Don't underestimate yourself because that is faith in action, whether it feels like it or not.

SEE THROUGH IT

When Israel stood between the Red Sea and Pharoah's advancing army, Moses gave them instructions from God. "Stand still and see the salvation of the Lord," he said. He didn't say, "Step into the water and see the salvation of the Lord." That would have made sense, but he told them to stand still.

When calamity is close, it is the human tendency to become frantic, but the instructions to Israel are a reminder that it is a calm faith, not a hyperactive frenzy, that is the order of the day. Stop struggling and stand still for whatever you're praying for in your life right now. Turn your attention to the Only One who can cause you to leap from the natural world to the supernatural world and see your circumstances through His eyes.

In 1873, Horatio Spafford planned to travel from America to Europe with his family on a ship. However, he had to stay back due to some unexpected business dealings and sent his family ahead without him.

Tragically, the ship his wife and daughters were on suffered a collision and sank. His four daughters did not survive the disaster.

.   .   .

Receiving the terrible news by telegraph while still in America, Spafford was grief-stricken. As he traveled to meet his bereaved wife, he was inspired to write these familiar words:

When peace, like a river, attendeth my way,
When sorrows like sea billows roll;
Whatever my lot, Thou hast taught me to say,
It is well, it is well with my soul.
Though Satan should buffet, though trials should
come,
Let this blest assurance control,
That Christ hath regarded my helpless estate,
And hath shed His own blood for my soul.
And, Lord, haste the day when my faith shall be
sight,
The clouds be rolled back as a scroll;
The trump shall resound, and the Lord shall
descend,
Even so, it is well with my soul. [2]

Look through the external and see the Eternal, then allow that to be the governing grace that establishes your internal state of being. In that moment, you will experience "peace that passes understanding." Quantum leaps don't make sense, but they are real. Christ will raise you to a higher level, above the temporal world of troubles, into the transcendent world of trust in Him. Watch Him, and you'll be fine.

WORK WITH IT

The blockade that blinds many people from seeing their prayers answered is that they struggle against the problems they have instead of working with them. That may sound strange, but it is a truth recognized medically and biblically. Many psychotherapy protocols emphasize confronting rather than avoiding difficult emotional experiences. "The only way out is through" is a phrase commonly used in these contexts.

To face our trials head-on is a biblical approach, too. James wrote, "Consider it pure joy, my brothers and sisters, whenever you face trials of many kinds because you know that the testing of your faith produces perseverance. Let perseverance finish its work so that you may be mature and complete, not lacking anything." (JAMES 1:2-4 NIV) The Apostle Paul said, "We also glory in our sufferings, because we know that suffering produces perseverance; perseverance, character; and character, hope. And hope does not put us to shame, because God's love has been poured out into our hearts through the Holy Spirit, who has been given to us." (ROMANS 5:3-5, NIV) In 1 Peter 5:10, the Apostle Peter affirmed, " And the God of all grace, who called you to his eternal glory in Christ, after you have suffered a little while, will himself restore you and make you strong, firm and steadfast."

To work with your problem is to realize the value embedded in it and to relate to it in the best way. Don't fear it but face it with confidence that you will pass through it and, in the end, be better because of it. Some of the worst situations we find ourselves in prove to have been pivotal moments in life when we look back on them in retrospect. Pray for grace to relate to your pain in a way that will work for your highest good. If you must endure the problem, at least don't waste it. Make it count for something by working together with it as you trust the One who can redeem any situation to utilize the process for good in your life. You may not be able to choose the details of your problem but you can choose how you relate to it.

TAKING THE LEAP

The most formidable way to fight fear with faith is to face it. Faith isn't a feeling you have but a choice you make. Let me use a personal example to illustrate how this works.

As I neared my sixty-seventh birthday a few years ago, I found myself thinking about how to have an experience that would take me beyond the boundaries of my comfort zone. I envisioned a challenge that would not only test me but also bring a different kind of sense of accomplishment.

The notion of skydiving was something I had occasionally thought about for a long time. When I discussed the idea with my wife, she immediately came on board with her support. I, on the other hand, was still undecided. Weeks passed, and the decision weighed on me—part exhilarating, part terrifying. I was caught in a limbo of indecision until, one day, my wife did something that people, who have been married as long as we have been, sometimes do. She decided for me.

Weeks before my birthday, she handed me a card containing a gift certificate for a tandem jump at Skydive City. Now it was settled. I was destined to ascend 13,500 feet above Earth, tethered to an instructor, and take the ultimate leap of faith.

The gift certificate's revelation left me with a severe sense of obligation. "Now I have to do it," I thought. "How can I renege now, especially when even my children and grandchildren know about the plan?" This was no longer a hypothetical—it was a commitment. And yet, fear wouldn't leave me alone.

Throughout countless flights, I'd heard pilots calmly announce that we were reaching a cruising altitude of 10,000 feet. Looking out the airplane window at those times, the world below seemed tiny, almost ant-like. Now, I was contemplating a jump from an altitude exceeding that by 3,500 feet. The thought both thrilled and unnerved me.

Every day, the anticipation consumed me. "Will I follow through or chicken out?" became a nightly rumination. It was a paradox: something I both desired and dreaded.

. . .

On the day of the jump, a mental shift occurred. It had to be that way. If I were to follow through, I knew a change in my mindset had to happen. So, I consciously chose to harness my fear and transform it into exhilarating enthusiasm.

"I'm ready for this!" I told myself and assured my family.

"You aren't scared?" I was asked.

"No, I'm psyched!" I honestly answered.

My confessions were working! I found myself becoming more and more excited about the jump. I wouldn't let myself think about it any other way.

When we arrived at the airfield, my instructor briefed me on the protocol. We boarded the airplane, he attached my harness to his own, and we took off. With each incremental rise in altitude, my excitement soared along with it. Finally, at 13,500 feet, it was time to jump. We maneuvered to the airplane's open door, my legs dangling in the great abyss.

"Are you ready?" my instructor queried.

. . .

"Let's rock!" I responded, feeling the surge of adrenaline.

We pushed ourselves from the plane, and for an electrifying sixty seconds, we free-fell at 120 mph. At the designated moment, I responded to my readiness to deploy the parachute with a thumbs-up in response to my instructor's prearranged thumbs-up. Upon its opening, we quickly slowed, spiraling gently downward in wide circles for another five minutes before touching down.

The experience was invigorating and liberating. It was my own "quantum leap" from fear to free-falling through the clouds with great enthusiasm. It was an unforgettable lesson, not only about skydiving and fear, but about every other situation in life that threatens to replace peace with anxiety.

Fear is faith pointed in the wrong direction. It is the expectation of a negative outcome. It is a mindset that can be taken under control and corrected by declining to be carried along by negative thinking and debilitating feelings. "Bring every thought into the captivity of Christ," the Bible admonishes. Quantum leaps in life happen when we take responsibility for ourselves and refuse to allow external influences to determine our outlook and outcomes.

Life often presents us with situations that feel scary and threatening, whether it's a health issue, a relationship struggle, financial problems, or any number of other challenges. Our natural tendency is to respond with fear and trepidation, which can leave us paralyzed and unable to move forward. But we have a choice. We can consciously shift our mindset from dread to determination, just as I did with my skydiving fears.

Quantum prayer is more than words. It is an action that empowers us to release the "what ifs" that plague our minds, and embrace faith— faith that He will equip us for whatever we face, faith that He has a purpose and plan in it all, and faith that we are not alone.

With our hearts and minds anchored in Him, we gain the confidence to take courageous action, to live by faith rather than fear. We find within ourselves the willingness to do the hard thing, take the risk, start the business, leave the unhealthy relationship, make the move, have the tough conversation, and so on. We may still feel the butterflies of nervousness, but we know we are not alone in facing them. God is by our side.

Take heart when you encounter an intimidating challenge. Don't let fear take root. Trust Him and boldly take the "leap of faith." He is tethered to you and will not let you go. The adventure may be scary, but you will safely land. On that, you can depend.

CONCLUSION

As we conclude our exploration of quantum prayer, it is my hope that you feel empowered to implement these scientific principles in your own prayer life. As you have seen, these truths are grounded in biblical teaching. My goal has been to provide you with practical ways to cooperate with the Spirit working in your circumstances. As physicist, John Wheeler noted, we live in a participatory universe. You are a co-laborer together with God. Approach prayer as a collaborative effort, joining forces with Him to bring about change. Have faith that your prayers set powerful forces in motion, even if you can't yet see the results.

God longs for you to experience Him in these deep places of quantum connection. He has placed eternity in your heart, and that divine realm is always accessible. Press in consistently and watch what unfolds, both internally and externally. Your life will never be the same. You'll gain new perspective, hope and strength.

May your courage and expectancy grow as you experience the unlimited potential of quantum prayer! As you stay tuned to His frequency, you'll find yourself living and loving on a whole new plane. One that is infused with meaning, purpose and the supernatural workings of our magnificent, limitless God.

Afterword

This is the third book in a series I've written from a quantum perspective. If you haven't read *Quantum Life* or *Quantum Faith*, you can get them on my Author's Page on Amazon by clicking this link - Steve McVey's Amazon Page

If you want to know more, you may be interested in an online subscription group I teach every weekday. In that community, we discuss practical ways to express grace in many areas of life. The teachings are available to watch at the viewers' convenience. It's a great group of people from diverse walks of life across the world. We would be happy to have you join us. You can get information about this community at www.gracewalkexperience.com. Additionally, you can find more complete information about all I do at www.stevemcvey.com.

Thank you for investing your time in this book. If you think others may benefit from it, I'd appreciate you helping promote it by posting a review on Amazon. May the Spirit of Truth continue to guide you into an ever-expanding knowledge of Life.

ENDNOTES

CHAPTER ONE

1. Eugene Wigner, "Remarks on the Mind-Body Question," in *Foundations of Quantum Mechanics*, ed. B. d'Espagnat (Academic Press, 1961), 47-66.
2. Amit Goswami, *The Self-Aware Universe: How Consciousness Creates the Material World* (Jeremy P. Tarcher/Perigee, 1993).
3. David Bohm, interview in *The Holographic Universe*, by Michael Talbot (1991).
4. Thomas Merton, *New Seeds of Contemplation* (New Directions Publishing, 2007), 120, chap. 9, "The General Dance."

CHAPTER TWO

1. Gregg Braden, *The Divine Matrix: Bridging Time, Space, Miracles, and Belief* (Hay House, Kindle Edition), 78-79.
2. J. Polkinghorne, "The Quantum World," *Nature* 474, no. 7350 (2011): 24-26.
3. Jennifer Ouellette, "What is Quantum Entanglement?" *Quanta Magazine*, 2018.
4. Frank Wilczek, *Fundamentals: Ten Keys to Reality* (Penguin Press, 2021).

CHAPTER THREE

1. Richard P. Feynman, *The Character of Physical Law* (The MIT Press, 2017), 129. Originally Messenger Lectures, Cornell University, 1964.
2. Sabine Hossenfelder, *Lost in Math: How Beauty Leads Physics Astray* (New York: Basic Books, 2018).
3. Max Planck, speech in Florence, Italy, 1944.

CHAPTER FOUR

1. Steve McVey, *Quantum Life* (Lodi, CA: The Writer's Society, 2023). I wrote extensively about this topic in *Quantum Life*. The power that resides where we place our attention is fundamental in shaping our life experiences.

2. C.S. Lewis, *Mere Christianity* (originally published in 1952; multiple editions available).`

CHAPTER SEVEN

Steve McVey, *Beyond an Angry God* (Eugene, OR: Harvest House Publishers, 2014).

CHAPTER EIGHT

1. T.S. Eliot, "East Coker," in *Four Quartets* (London: Faber and Faber, 1943), III.
2. Andrew Louth, *Discerning the Mystery: An Essay on the Nature of Theology* (Oxford: Clarendon Press, 1989).
3. Søren Kierkegaard, in *Papers and Journals: A Selection*, ed. Alastair Hannay (London: Penguin Classics, 1996), 160.

CHAPTER NINE

1. Augustine, *The Confessions of Saint Augustine*, Book II, Chapter 6, trans. E.B. Pusey (1907).
2. G. Binnig et al., "Tunneling through a controllable vacuum gap," *Applied Physics Letters* 40, no. 2 (1982): 178-180.
3. T.C.L.G. Sollner et al., "Resonant tunneling through quantum wells at frequencies up to 2.5 THz," *Applied Physics Letters* 43, no. 6 (1983): 588-590.

4. J. Basran, E.J. Sutcliffe, and N.S. Scrutton, "Enzymes can work in tunneling conditions," *Biochemistry* 38, no. 16 (1999): 5043-5048.

CHAPTER TEN

1. "New Features of the Franck-Hertz Experiment," *American Journal of Physics* 74, no. 5 (2006).
2. Horatio G. Spafford, "It Is Well With My Soul" (Public domain hymn, 1873).

ENDORSEMENTS

WHAT OTHERS HAVE SAID ABOUT STEVE McVEY'S BOOKS:

Sixteen Grammy Award Winning Gospel Singer, Kirk Franklin said, "Steve McVey's books have been used by God to transform my Christian walk."

Fourteen Grammy Award winner, Ron Block wrote, "Steve McVey is one of the voices unafraid to tell the whole truth about grace. Steve's biblical, solid, and life-changing writing points me to the freely-given love, favor, and grace of God in Christ - a grace walk experience."

Dr. Tony Evans, President of The Urban Alternative wrote, "My good friend, Steve McVey, has put the amazing back into grace."

Gary Smalley, author of *The Language of Love*: "Few people have had the life change effect on my life that Steve McVey has had. Whenever I hear that he has a new book, I buy several copies."

Neil Anderson, author of The Bondage Breaker: "(Steve McVey's book) *A Divine Invitation* will enlarge your heart and increase your comprehension of God's love that goes beyond knowledge."

The late Bill Bright, Founder of Campus Crusade for Christ, wrote about *A Divine Invitation*: "Steve McVey has given us in very clear and understandable language a wonderful, indelible picture of just how beautiful, complete and even startling God's love for us really is."

ABOUT THE AUTHOR

Dr. Steve McVey is the author of twenty-one books, including the best seller, *Grace Walk*. Steve writes to address specific needs in the reader's life. His books are filled with biblical truth, practical application, humor and affirmation that will encourage you and strengthen you in your own journey of faith.

Steve and his wife, Melanie, live in the Tampa Bay area of Florida. They have four adult children and five grandchildren.

ALSO BY STEVE MCVEY

Grace Walk

The Secret of Grace

Grace Amazing

52 Lies Heard in Church Every Sunday

Grace Walk Devotional

Helping Other Overcome Addictions (with Mike Quarles)

Unlock Your Bible

A Divine Invitation

Walking in the Will of God

When Wives Walk in Grace

The Godward Gaze

Grace Walk Moments

Getting Past the Hurt (with Melanie McVey)

Beyond an Angry God

The Grace Walk Experience Workbook

Journey into Intimacy Workbook

Anchored: Five Keys to a Secure Faith

Quantum Life

Quantum Faith

Butterfly Kisses (children's book)

Made in the USA
Coppell, TX
04 October 2023

22415327R00083